Donna Kooler's
Glorious
Needlepoint

STERLING PUBLISHING CO., INC. NEW YORK
A STERLING/CHAPELLE BOOK

For Kooler Design Studio, Inc.

President
> Donna Kooler

Executive Vice President
> Linda Gillum

Executive Assistant
> Loretta Heden

Senior Designer
> Nancy Rossi

Staff Designers
> Barbara Baatz
> Holly DeFount
> Jorja Hernandez
> Sandy Orton

Creative Director
> Deanna Hall West

Project Director
> Priscilla Timm

Design Assistants
> Sara Angle
> Anita Forfang
> Laurie Grant
> Virginia Hanley-Rivett
> Marsha Hinkson
> Arlis Johnson
> Lori Patton
> Char Randolph
> Gina Shaw
> Michele O'Connor
> Pam Whyte

Framers
> Frame City, Pleasant Hill, CA
> Artist Touch, Ogden, Ut

For Chapelle Ltd.

Owner
> Jo Packham

Editorial
> Amanda Beth McPeck
> Leslie Ridenour

Staff
> Malissa Boatwright
> Rebecca Christensen
> Amber Hansen
> Holly Hollingsworth
> Susan Jorgensen
> Susan Laws
> Barbara Milburn
> Pat Pearson
> Cindy Rooks
> Cindy Stoeckl
> Nancy Whitley

Photography
> Kevin Dilley for Hazen Photography

Photography Styling
> Cherie Herrick

If you have any questions or comments or would like information on specialty products featured in this book, please contact:

Chapelle Ltd., Inc.
PO Box 9252
Ogden, UT 84409
(801) 621-2777
(801) 621-2788 (fax)

Library of Congress Cataloging-in-Publication Data

Kooler, Donna.
   [Glorious needlepoint]
   Donna Kooler's glorious needlepoint.
     p.   cm.
   "A Sterling/Chapelle book."
   Includes index.
   ISBN 0-8069-3152-3
     1. Canvas embroidery—Patterns.
I. Title.
   TT778.C3K6623   1996
   746.44'2'041—dc20   96-19457
                       CIP

10 9 8 7 6 5 4 3 2 1

Published by Sterling Publishing Company, Inc.
387 Park Avenue South, New York, N.Y. 10016
© 1996 by Chapelle Limited
Distributed in Canada by Sterling Publishing
c/o Canadian Manda Group, One Atlantic Avenue,
Suite 105, Toronto, Ontario, Canada M6K 3E7
Distributed in Great Britain and Europe by Cassell PLC
Wellington House, 125 Strand, London WC2R 0BB,
England
Distributed in Australia by Capricorn Link (Australia) Pty
Ltd., P.O. Box 6651, Baulkham Hills, Business Centre, NSW
2153, Australia

Printed and Bound in Hong Kong

Sterling ISBN 0-8069-3152-3

Needlework is not only my profession—it is also my pleasure. For the past 25 years I have experienced a sense of accomplishment and satisfaction in working with fibers, fabrics, color, and especially good design. Although I enjoy all the various needle arts, my first love has always been needlepoint. This book is the fruit of that love of classic needlepoint in its purest form—designs without decorative stitches or exotic fibers. These creations, when stitched, will enter into that timeless realm of heirlooms by the sheer excellence of their design.

With the 10-year establishment of Kooler Design Studio, Inc., I've had the fortunate opportunity to gather together the crème de la crème of American needlework designers. Many of these designers have contributed to this needlepoint collection.

I hope this book will excite the creative needs of the novice and expert alike, for each completed project will be a reflection of the stitcher's own style by the way the design is finished and the surroundings in which it is placed. Each needlepoint creation is destined to become a coveted family treasure to be enjoyed for years to come.

—*Donna Kooler*

DESIGNS AND DESIGNERS

Barbara Baatz
Primrose Path, Victorian Flora & Fauna, Victorian Butterfly, Kriss Kringle, Golden Trout Pond, Bountiful Harvest, and Cabbage Roses

Linda Gillum
Lotsa Puppies

Jorja Hernandez
Vintage Vines

Sandy Orton
Colonial Sampler and Colonial Alphabet

Nancy Rossi
Père Noël, Father Christmas, St. Nicholas, Santa Claus, Fleur-de-lis, Woodland Rabbit, Hens & Chicks, Summer Concerto, Golden Tassels and Christmas Elegance

KOOLER
DESIGN
STUDIO
INC.

Contents

General Information

Canvas

The traditional background fabric used for needlepoint is canvas. Canvas is made of cotton threads woven with spaces between the threads. It is treated with a substance called "sizing," which acts to stiffen, strengthen and smooth the woven fibers for easier stitching.

Canvas is categorized by the number of threads per inch. This is also called the "gauge" of the canvas. For example, a 10-mesh canvas has 10 threads in one inch. Intersections of crossing canvas threads are called "meshes." As the number of mesh increases, the threads are closer and the stitches are smaller.

Mono Standard Canvas 13

Petit Point 22

Interlock Canvas 13

Double Mesh "Penelope" 10

Linen Canvas 17

Interlock Canvas 7

Mono Canvas 18

Tan Bargello 13

Some canvases used for needlepoint.

Mounting Frames

To hold the canvas taut while working the design, mount on a stretcher or scroll frame. A stretcher frame consists of four strips of wood joined to form a rectangle, similar to a picture frame. A scroll frame is an adjustable wooden frame consisting of two rollers with webbing attached and two strips of wood which hold the rollers at the desired distance.

Finished Design Size

Finished design sizes are given for canvas used in sample and for 10-, 12-, 13-, 14-, and 18-count canvases. To determine size of finished design on canvas other than those listed, divide stitch count by number of threads per inch of canvas.

Centering Design

Fold canvas in half horizontally, then vertically. Place a pin in the fold point to mark the center. Locate the center of the design on the graph by following the vertical and horizontal arrows in the left and bottom margins. Begin stitching all designs at the center point of the graph and the canvas, unless otherwise indicated.

Needles

Use a tapestry needle to work needlepoint or cross-stitch. This type of needle has a blunt point and a large eye. The blunt point will not split the canvas threads and the large eye will accommodate thick yarn. The needle size depends on the gauge of canvas.

Use a #18 tapestry needle for 10 mesh. Use a #20 for 12 and 14 mesh. Use a #22 for 14 and 18 mesh. A #24 can also be used for 18 mesh.

Graphs & Color Codes

Each grid square on the graphs in this book represents one stitch to be worked. When stitching on canvas, each grid square equals one canvas thread intersection or mesh.

Each color and symbol found on the graph corresponds to a specific color of fiber, identified on the color code which accompanies the graph. Fibers are cross-referenced, giving both Paternayan Persian Yarn and DMC embroidery floss color numbers.

The steps in the color code indicate stitches to be used and number of strands for each stitch.

Fibers

PERSIAN YARN

This yarn is made up of three strands of wool loosely twisted together. Strands can be used alone or can be combined as necessary to cover canvas.

TAPESTRY YARN

This yarn is a single-stranded wool that is about the same thickness as the three-stranded Persian yarn. It cannot be separated into thinner strands and is usually used on 10- and 12-mesh canvas.

PEARL COTTON

This is a shiny single-strand thread which comes in different thicknesses.

EMBROIDERY FLOSS

A six-stranded thread made up of a shiny cotton, it can be separated into strands. The strands are then combined to form a thread of exact thickness to cover canvas. The sheen and colors produce a fine finish to the work.

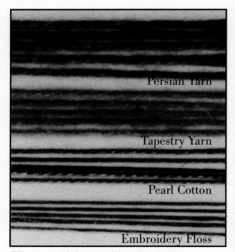

Persian Yarn

Tapestry Yarn

Pearl Cotton

Embroidery Floss

Fibers used for needlepoint.

Stitching Method

STAB-STITCHING

Use the Stab Stitch method on stretched canvas by pushing needle up through canvas in one motion and going down through canvas in a second motion. Work with one hand above the canvas and one hand below it to guide the needle in and out of the canvas.

BEGINNING, ENDING & CARRYING THREAD

Use 18" lengths for easy management of yarns and threads. Begin a new thread by making a knot at the end of the fiber. Push needle down through canvas about an inch away from point where first stitch will be made and along line of first line of stitches. The knot will be on the front of the canvas. Come up through the canvas at the point of the first stitch and begin working line. While working toward the knot, stitches will be worked over the tail of the yarn on the back. Upon reaching the knot, snip it off close to the canvas and continue working design.

Begin a new thread in an area that has been partially worked by running needle through backs of a few nearby stitches. Pull the thread through until the end of the tail just disappears under the stitch backs and proceed with stitching.

End the thread by running needle through back of existing stitches and cut close to canvas.

Do not carry thread across any fabric that is not yet or will not be stitched. Do not carry thread more than three or four meshes in the back if going from one area of the design to another. Run needle under stitches on the back of canvas for short distances when fiber colors are similar. Otherwise, end the thread and restart it in the new area.

Stitches

TENT—CONTINENTAL STITCH

Work from right to left in horizontal rows or top to bottom in vertical columns, making small diagonal stitches over one intersection or mesh. The back side of stitching will result in long slanting stitches.

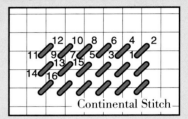

Continental Stitch

STRAIGHT STITCH

This stitch can be taut or loose, depending on desired effect. Come up and go down upon achieving desired length.

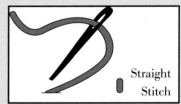

Straight Stitch

OUTLINE STITCH

Bring the needle out at the end of the line at 1. Keep the thread to the right and above the needle. Push needle down at 2 and back up at 3.

Outline Stitch

COUCHED YARN & THREAD

Complete a Straight Stitch the

desired length of the design. Make sure yarn/thread is flat.

Make short tight Straight Stitches across base to "couch" the Straight Stitch (1-2). Come up on one side of the thread (3). Go down on the opposite side of the thread (4). Tack at varying intervals.

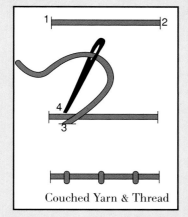
Couched Yarn & Thread

BACKSTITCH

Complete all needlework or cross-stitches before working backstitches or other accent stitches. Work from right to left with one strand (unless otherwise indicated). Bring needle up at 1, down at 2, and up at 3. Going back down at 1, continue.

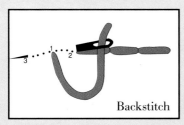
Backstitch

LONG LOOSE STITCH

This stitch consists of Straight Stitches worked over two or more threads traveling across fabric. Secure thread by running ends through existing stitches on back. Come up at starting point from wrong side of fabric and go down at ending point.

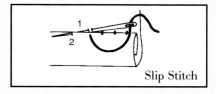
Long Loose Stitch

FRENCH KNOT

Bring needle up at 1. Wrap fiber around needle twice (unless otherwise indicated). Insert needle at 2, pulling fiber until it fits snugly around needle. Pull needle through to back.

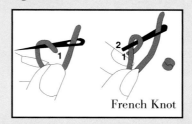
French Knot

STAR BUTTON & BELL PLACEMENT

Using one strand of floss, come up through canvas. Slide the button or bell on the needle and push the needle back down through canvas. Knot off each button or bell.

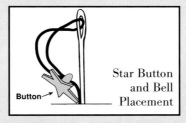
Button →
Star Button and Bell Placement

BINDING STITCH

Finish edges of canvas by following numbering in diagram. Work only on edge of canvas. Use two threads of the canvas to secure it properly.

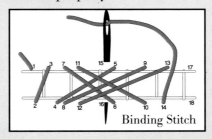
Binding Stitch

SLIP STITCH

Use this stitch to secure folded edges of fabric together or folded edge to base fabric. Insert needle at 1, taking a small stitch, and slide it through the folded edge of the fabric about ⅛" to ¼", bringing it out at 2.

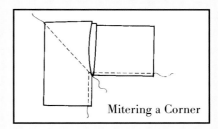
Slip Stitch

Mitering a Corner

Sew border strips up to, but not through, the seam allowance; backstitch. Repeat on all four edges, making stitching lines meet exactly at the corners. Fold two adjacent border pieces together. Mark; then stitch at a 45-degree angle. Trim seam allowance to ¼".

Mitering a Corner

Blocking

Stretch and shape finished piece right side up and pin in place on covered piece of cardboard. Spray with cold water from a fine-mist spray bottle until damp. Allow to dry away from direct sunlight or heat. A warm atmosphere is best for drying.

Cleaning

If canvas is colorfast, wash finished piece using a special detergent for needlework, following manufacturer's instructions. If it is not colorfast, have the piece dry-cleaned.

Converting Needlepoint to Cross-Stitch

Although counted thread styles of embroidery are not the main emphasis of this book, the graphs can also be used for counted cross-stitching on even-weave fabrics. The graph at right is a section of the Santa Claus design on page 91 which was used to complete both the pillow in needlepoint on canvas (pictured center right), and the framed piece in counted cross-stitch on even-weave fabric (pictured lower right).

When cross-stitching on even-weave fabric, each grid square represents one cross-stitch. As in needlepoint canvases, even-weave fabrics vary in thread counts per inch. This determines the size of the finished design. The larger the thread count per inch, the smaller the finished design size. Some different types of fabric will produce the same finished design size. For example, an Aida 14-count fabric yields 14 stitches per inch. Respectively, a linen 28-count fabric also yields 14 stitches per inch when stitched over two threads.

FABRICS

Some examples of fabrics used for counted cross-stitching over one interlocked group of threads are Aida 14, Aida 16 and Aida 18. Linen 32, 28, 25, and Murano 30, Linda 27, and Lugana 25 are some examples of fabrics used when stitching over two threads.

FINISHED DESIGN SIZE

Determine the finished design size using the same method used with canvas. When the design is stitched over two threads, divide the stitch count by half the number of threads per inch.

EMBROIDERY FLOSS

Most counted cross-stitch is worked with six-strand embroidery floss. Use two strands for cross-stitches and one strand for backstitching or outlining. See photo on page 6.

NEEDLES

Use a #24 tapestry needle for 11-count fabrics. Use a #24 or #26 for 14-count. Use a #26 for 18-count.

CROSS-STITCH

Come up at 1. Go down at 2. Come up at 3 and go down at 4, forming an "X". Make half-cross by coming up at 3 at midpoint of 1-2 stitch. Stitch rows as shown.

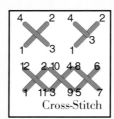

8

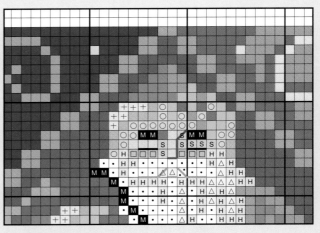

Santa Claus graph section.

Santa Claus stitched on canvas using needlepoint method.

Santa Claus stitched on even-weave using cross-stitch method.

Spring

Victorian Flora & Fauna

Pillow

Stitched on 12-mesh canvas, the finished design size is 12¼" x 12¼". The stitch count is 141 x 136. The canvas was cut 18" x 18".

OTHER CANVASES	DESIGN SIZES
10 count	14⅛" x 13⅝"
13 count	10⅞" x 10½"
14 count	10⅛" x 9¾"
18 count	7⅞" x 7½"

DMC — Paternayan Persian Yarn (used for sample)

Step 1: Continental Stitch (2 ply)

DMC		Paternayan	
White	·	260	White
3823		755	Old Gold–vy. lt.
3822	+	727	Autumn Yellow–ultra vy. lt.
977		723	Autumn Yellow–med.
754		490	Flesh–dk.
3779	∴	486	Terra-cotta–vy. lt.
743	△	815	Sunrise–vy. lt.
740		812	Sunrise–med.
351		843	Salmon
3801	N	841	Salmon–dk.
347		968	Christmas Red–vy. dk.
902		900	American Beauty–ultra vy. dk.
819	○	326	Plum–vy. lt.
3689	s	907	American Beauty–ultra vy. lt.
604		905	American Beauty–lt.
601	★	903	American Beauty–med.
211	□	314	Grape–vy. lt.
3746		332	Lavender
3747	U	344	Periwinkle–vy. lt.
793	E	342	Periwinkle
333		340	Periwinkle–dk.
772	×	695	Loden Green–vy. lt.
3348		694	Loden Green–lt.
3347		693	Loden Green
3346		692	Loden Green–med.
504		664	Pine Green–lt.
562		663	Pine Green
561	♥	661	Pine Green–dk.
500		660	Pine Green–vy. dk.
310	M	220	Black

Step 2: Couched Thread (DMC Floss 3 strands)

 310 Black

Top Left

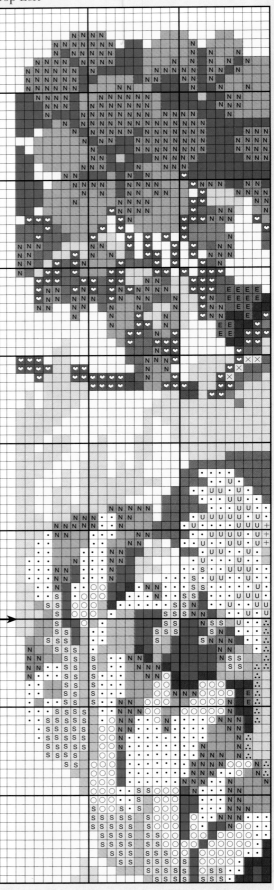

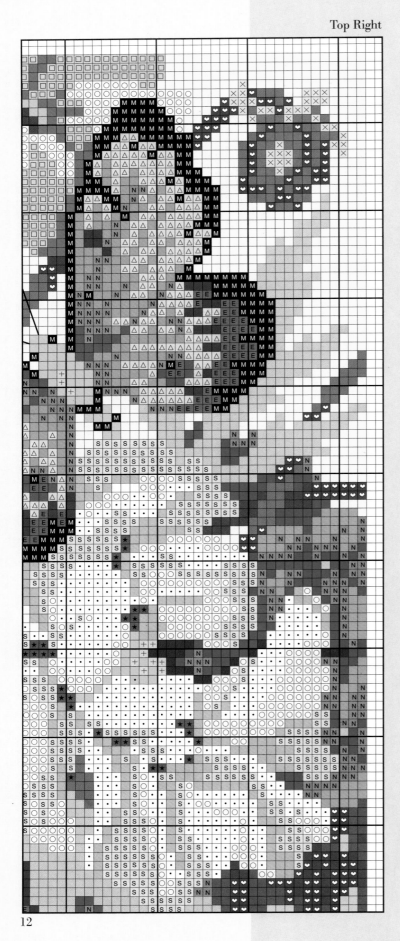

Pillow Finishing

MATERIALS

Completed design on 12-mesh canvas
½ yard of gold moiré decorator-weight fabric; matching thread
2 yards of 1¾"-wide matching decorative trim with fringe
12"-square pillow form

DIRECTIONS
All seams are ½".

1. Trim canvas ½" from last row of stitches.

2. Cut four 3" x 18" strips of fabric for borders on front of pillow. Cut one 17"-square piece of fabric for back of pillow.

3. With right sides together, baste and sew a fabric strip to each side of design, mitering corners. Trim excess fabric from mitered corners. Press seams flat.

4. Baste and sew decorative trim to front of pillow next to seams, mitering the trim at the corners.

5. With right sides together, baste and sew pillow front and fabric for back of pillow together, leaving a 5" opening for turning. Trim corners. Turn right side out.

6. Insert pillow form into pillow. Slip-stitch opening closed.

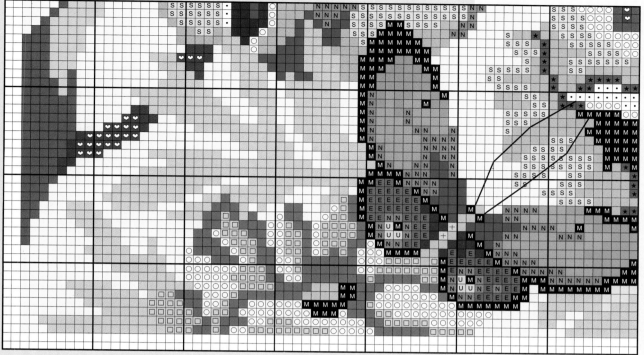

Bottom Left

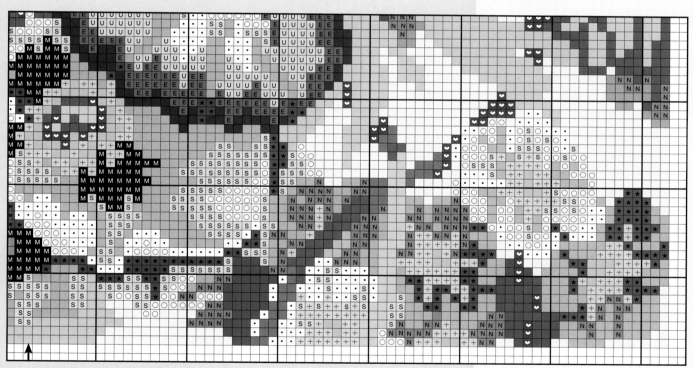

Bottom Right

Pincushion

See photo on page 15. Stitched on 18-mesh canvas, the finished design size is 3½" x 3½". The stitch count is 64 x 64. The canvas was cut 10" x 10". The code and graph are on page 14. See "Pincushion Finishing" instructions on page 14.

OTHER CANVASES	DESIGN SIZES
10 count	6⅜" x 6⅜"
12 count	5⅜" x 5⅜"
13 count	4⅞" x 4⅞"
14 count	4⅝" x 4⅝"

DMC		Paternayan Persian Yarn (used for sample)	
Step 1:		Continental Stitch (1 ply)	
743		815	Sunrise–vy. lt.
740		812	Sunrise–med.
977	★	723	Autumn Yellow–med.
351		843	Salmon
3801	△	841	Salmon–dk.
347		968	Christmas Red–vy. dk.
819	□	326	Plum–vy. lt.
3689		907	American Beauty–ultra vy. lt.
604		905	American Beauty–lt.
211	·	314	Grape–vy. lt.
3746		332	Lavender
793	N	342	Periwinkle

DMC			
333		340	Periwinkle–dk.
772	○	695	Loden Green–vy. lt.
3348		694	Loden Green–lt.
3347		693	Loden Green
504		664	Pine Green–lt.
562		663	Pine Green
561	♥	661	Pine Green–dk.
500		660	Pine Green–vy. dk.
310	M	220	Black

Step 2:		Couched Yarn (1 ply)	
310	┼	220	Black (antenna)

MATERIALS

Completed design on 18-mesh canvas

½ yard of 1"-wide purple ombré wired ribbon

¼ yard of purple velvet decorator-weight fabric; matching thread

⅛ yard muslin fabric

Decorative pins

Polyester stuffing

Pincushion

DIRECTIONS
All seams are ½".

1. Trim canvas ½" from last row of stitches.

2. Cut a 3½" x 28" strip of velvet fabric for gathered edge of cushion. Cut a 3" x 15" strip of muslin fabric for lining of gathered edge. Cut one 4½"-square piece of velvet fabric for base of cushion.

3. Gather-stitch both long edges of velvet strip. Pull gathers until strip is approximately 15" long. With wrong sides together, baste and sew gathered edges of velvet strip to muslin strip, aligning the long raw edges and distributing gathers evenly. The velvet strip will be slightly wider than the muslin and will balloon out.

4. With right sides together, baste and sew one edge of gathered strip to the design next to stitching, rounding corners slightly. Turn short raw edges of velvet strip under, overlapping one over the other.

5. With right sides together, baste and sew remaining edge of gathered strip of the cushion base, leaving a 1" opening for turning. Trim corners. Turn right side out.

6. Stuff with polyester stuffing. Slip-stitch opening on gathered edge closed.

7. Tie a bow with ribbon. Attach to cushion with decorative pins.

Primrose Path

Stitched on 10-mesh canvas, the finished design size is 14½" x 14⅜". The stitch count is 145 x 144. The canvas was cut 20" x 20".

OTHER CANVASES	DESIGN SIZES
12 count	12⅛" x 12"
13 count	11⅛" x 11⅛"
14 count	10⅜" x 10⅜"
18 count	8⅛" x 8"

DMC   Paternayan Persian Yarn (used for sample)

Step 1: Continental Stitch (2 ply)

DMC				
712		261	Off White	
445		714	Mustard–lt.	
744	○	703	Butterscotch–lt.	
742		814	Sunrise–lt.	
971	✕	801	Marigold–dk.	
921		880	Ginger–vy. dk.	
3756	+	507	Federal Blue–ultra vy. lt.	
827		554	Ice Blue–lt.	
322		502	Federal Blue–dk.	
3348		694	Loden Green–lt.	
3347	N	693	Loden Green	
988		612	Hunter Green–med.	
987		611	Hunter Green–dk.	
561	★	661	Pine Green–dk.	
500		660	Pine Green–vy. dk.	
422	△	442	Golden Brown–med.	
869		441	Golden Brown–dk.	
839		461	Beige Brown–med.	

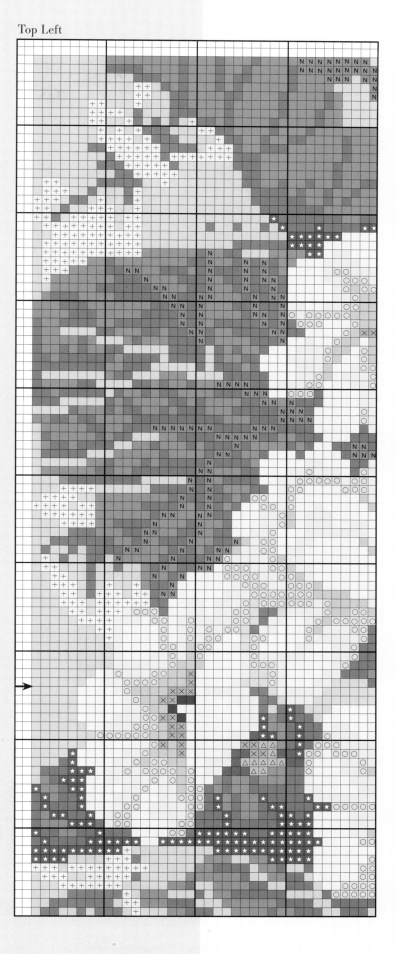

Top Center

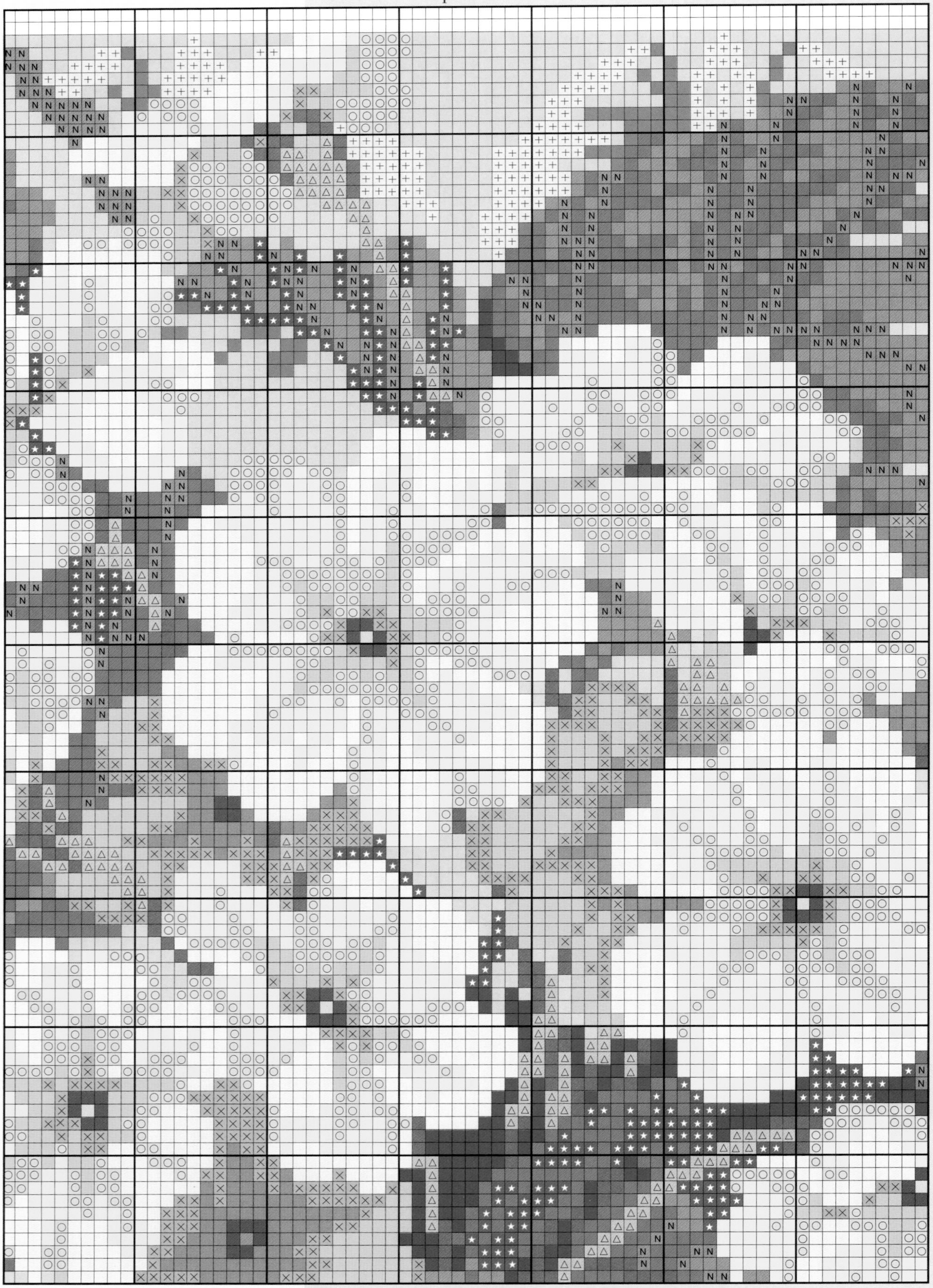

Pillow Finishing

MATERIALS

Completed design on 10-mesh canvas

½ yard of blue decorator-weight fabric; matching thread

1⅔ yards of ⅜"-diameter blue-and-gold twisted cording with lip

14"-square pillow form

DIRECTIONS

All seams are ½".

1. Trim canvas ½" from last row of stitches.

2. Using design canvas as a pattern, cut a piece of decorator fabric for pillow back.

3. Baste and sew cording around edges of stitching, overlapping ends at the center bottom and rounding corners slightly.

4. With right sides together, baste and sew pillow front and back together, leaving a 7" opening for turning. Trim corners and turn right side out.

5. Insert pillow form into pillow. Slip-stitch opening closed.

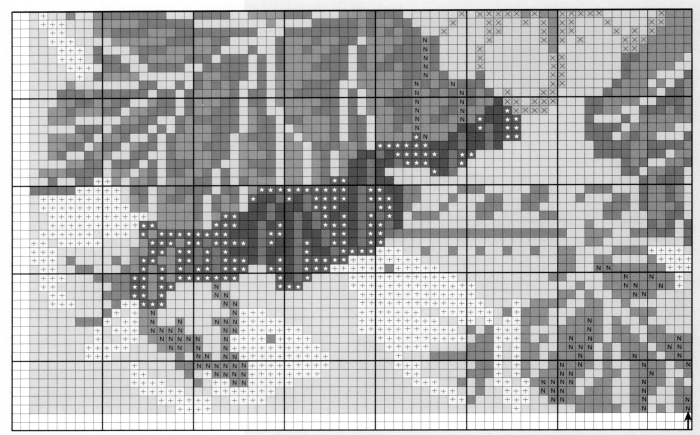

Bottom Left

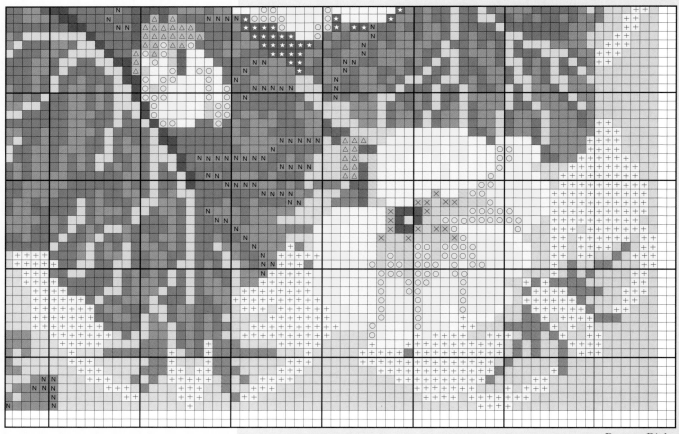

Bottom Right

Woodland Rabbit

Stitched on 12-mesh canvas, the finished design size is 14⅛" x 12¼". The stitch count is 168 x 144. The canvas was cut 20" x 18".

OTHER CANVASES	DESIGN SIZES
10 count	16¾" x 14⅜"
13 count	12⅞" x 11⅛"
14 count	12" x 10¼"
18 count	9⅜" x 8"

DMC		Paternayan Persian Yarn (used for sample)	
Step 1:	Continental Stitch (2 ply)		
White	·	260	White
744		703	Butterscotch–lt.
963		946	Cranberry–lt.
776	○	945	Cranberry
760		933	Rusty Rose
224	⁛	923	Wood Rose
962	s	904	American Beauty
3726		912	Dusty Pink–med.
3743	☐	334	Lavender–vy. lt.

Top Left

209		313	Grape–lt.	
3608		322	Plum–dk.	
550		311	Grape–med.	
3747		344	Periwinkle–vy. lt.	
341		343	Periwinkle–lt.	
794	×	561	Glacier–med.	
772		695	Loden Green–vy. lt.	
3348	△	694	Loden Green–lt.	
369	–	614	Hunter Green–lt.	
966		613	Hunter Green	
988		612	Hunter Green–med.	
368		604	Forest Green –lt.	
3363	H	603	Forest Green	
3362		601	Forest Green–dk.	
3815	❤	662	Pine Green–med.	

500		660	Pine Green–vy. dk.	
754		490	Flesh–dk.	
922		884	Ginger–lt.	
3826		883	Ginger	
920	N	882	Ginger–med.	
840		433	Chocolate Brown–med.	
801		432	Chocolate Brown–dk.	
838	★	460	Beige Brown–dk.	
310	E	220	Black	

Step 2: Couched Yarn (1 ply)

White	⌡	260	White
3348	⌡	694	Loden Green–lt.

MATERIALS

Completed design on 12-mesh
  canvas
½ yard of grape decorator-weight
  fabric; matching thread
1½ yards of ⅜"-diameter grape
  twisted cording with lip
14" x 12" pillow form or polyester
  stuffing

(continued on page 24)

Top Center

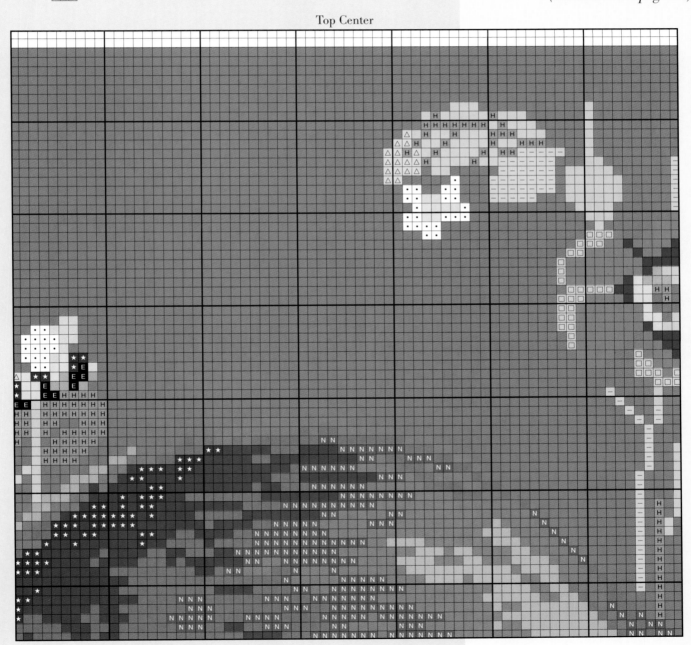

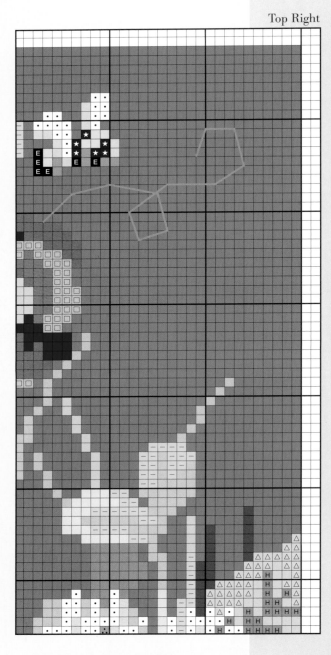

Bottom Left

(continued from page 23)

DIRECTIONS
All seams are ½".

1. Trim canvas ½" from last row of stitches.

2. Using design canvas as a pattern, cut a piece of decorator fabric for pillow back.

3. Baste and sew cording around edges of stitching, overlapping

ends at the center bottom and rounding corners slightly.

4. With right sides together, baste and sew pillow front and back together, leaving a 7"

opening for turning. Trim corners. Turn right side out.

5. Insert pillow form into pillow or stuff with polyester stuffing. Slip-stitch opening closed.

24

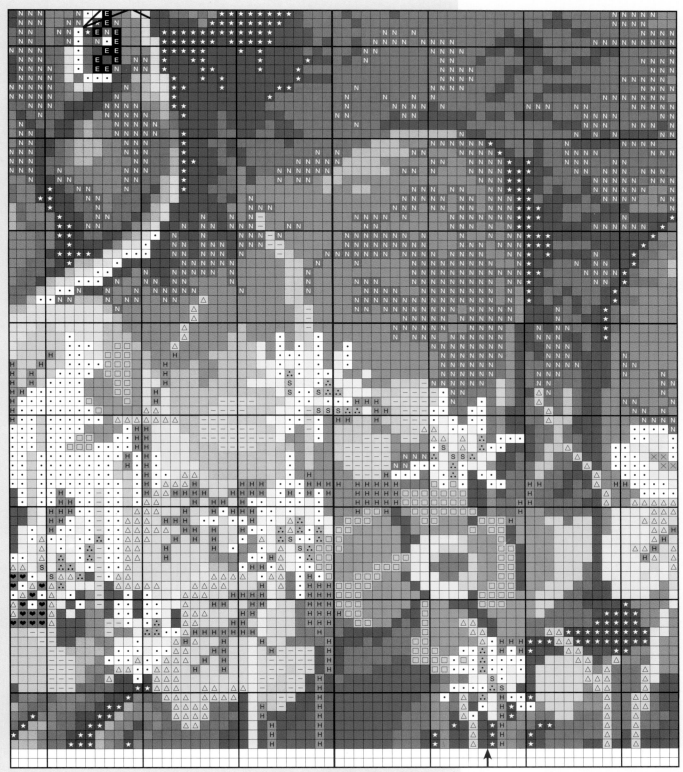

Bottom Center

Bottom Right

Hen & Chicks

Stitched on 12-mesh canvas, the finished design size is 14¼" x 12¼". The stitch count is 167 x 144. The canvas was cut 20" x 18".

OTHER CANVASES	DESIGN SIZES
10 count	16¾" x 14⅜"
13 count	12⅞" x 11⅛"
14 count	11⅞" x 10¼"
18 count	9¼" x 8"

DMC		Paternayan Persian Yarn (used for sample)
		Step 1: Continental Stitch (2 ply)
712		261 Off White
3078		716 Mustard–ultra vy. lt.
445	○	714 Mustard–lt.
3822	+	727 Autumn Yellow–ultra vy. lt.
783		724 Autumn Yellow
977		723 Autumn Yellow–med.
677	△	735 Honey Gold–vy. lt.
676		734 Honey Gold–lt.

DMC		Paternayan
402		855 Spice–vy. lt.
722	/	854 Spice–lt.
741	N	802 Marigold–med.
351		843 Salmon
946	S	820 Tangerine–vy. dk.
356		931 Rusty Rose–dk.
355	★	930 Rusty Rose–vy. dk.
778		915 Dusty Pink–vy. lt.
316		913 Dusty Pink
315		911 Dusty Pink–dk.
3743	□	334 Lavender–vy. lt.

Top Left

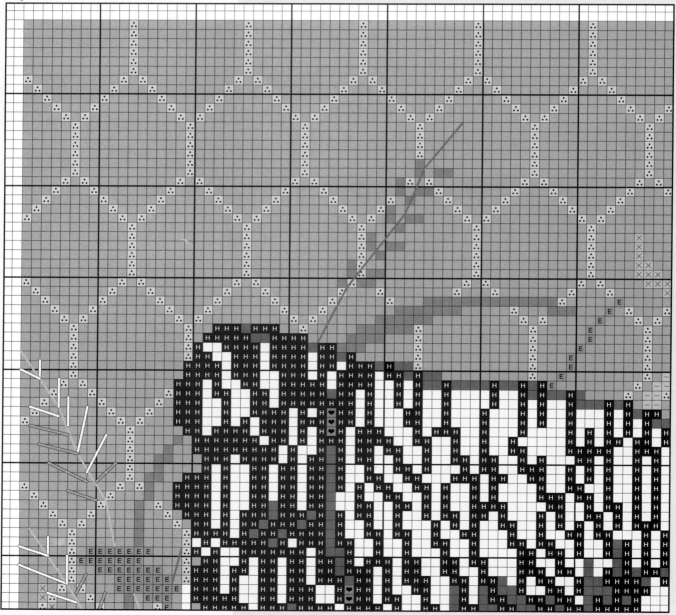

210		333	Lavender–lt.
208		312	Grape
472		654	Olive Green–lt.
3013	×	653	Olive Green
3012	E	652	Olive Green–med.
368		604	Forest Green–lt.
3363	•	603	Forest Green
3362		601	Forest Green–dk.
422	–	442	Golden Brown–med.
420		424	Coffee Brown–vy. lt.
318		202	Steel Gray
414	♥	200	Steel Gray–dk.
310	H	220	Black

Step 2: Couched Thread (1 ply)

422		442	Golden Brown–med.
869		869	Hazel Nut Brown–vy. dk. (DMC Floss 2 strands)

Step 3: Straight Stitch (2 ply)

3078	/	716	Mustard–ultra vy. lt.
3822	/	727	Autumn Yellow–ultra vy. lt.
677	/	735	Honey Gold–vy. lt.

Step 4: Backstitch (1 ply)

310	⌐	220	Black

Pillow Finishing

MATERIALS

Completed design on 12-mesh canvas

½ yard grape decorator-weight fabric; matching thread

1½ yards of ⅜"-diameter grape twisted cord with lip

14" x 12" pillow form or polyester stuffing

(continued on page 30)

Top Center

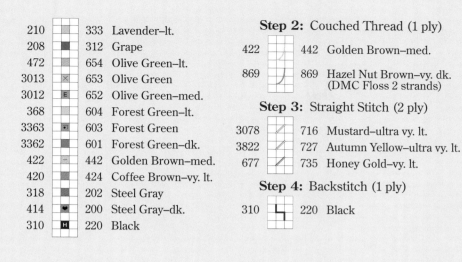

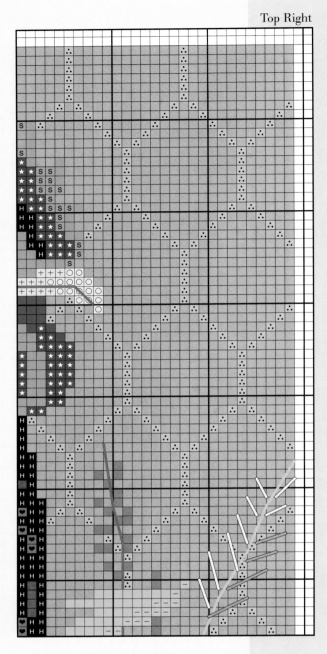

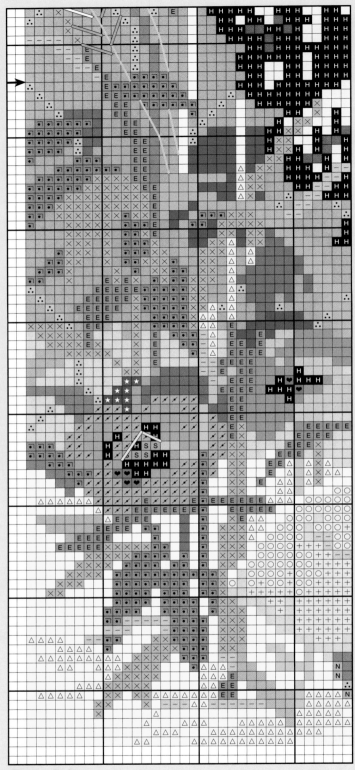

Bottom Left

(continued from page 29)

DIRECTIONS
All seams are ½".

1. Trim canvas ½" from last row of stitches.

2. Using design canvas as a pattern, cut a piece of decorator fabric for pillow back.

3. Baste and sew cording around edges of stitching, overlapping

30

ends at the center bottom and rounding corners slightly.

4. With right sides together, baste and sew pillow front and back together, leaving a 7"

opening for turning. Trim corners. Turn right side out.

5. Insert pillow form into pillow or stuff with polyester stuffing. Slip-stitch opening closed.

Bottom Center

Bottom Right

Summer

Cabbage Roses

Stitched on 12-mesh canvas, the finished design size is 19½" x 10½". The stitch count is 238 x 125. The canvas was cut 24" x 15".

OTHER CANVASES	DESIGN SIZES
10 count	23¾" x 12½"
13 count	18¼" x 9⅝"
14 count	17" x 8⅞"
18 count	13¼" x 7"

Top Left

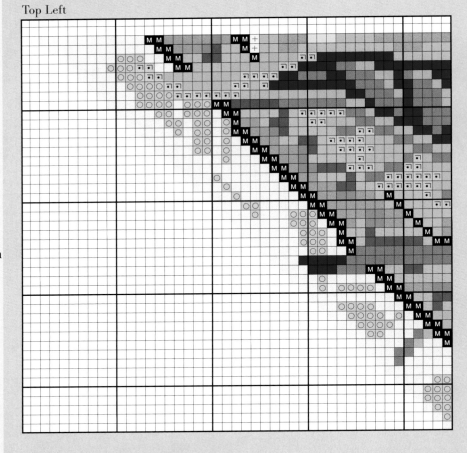

DMC		Paternayan Persian Yarn (used for sample)	
Step 1: Continental Stitch (2 ply)			
712	·	261	Off White
746	+	715	Mustard–vy. lt.
3822		727	Autumn Yellow–ultra vy. lt.
783		724	Autumn Yellow
977		723	Autumn Yellow–med.
353	×	835	Bittersweet–vy. lt.
3340		844	Salmon–lt.
351		843	Salmon
963	□	946	Cranberry–lt.
776		945	Cranberry
3708	★	944	Cranberry–med.
335		942	Cranberry–vy. dk.
326		940	Cranberry–deep
3747	○	344	Periwinkle–vy. lt.
3817		523	Teal Blue
966		613	Hunter Green
3346		612	Hunter Green–med.
986		610	Hunter Green–vy. dk.
762		237	Silver Gray
310	M	220	Black

Pillow Finishing

MATERIALS

Completed design on 12-mesh canvas
½ yard of blue velvet upholstery-weight fabric; matching thread
1½ yards of ⅜"-diameter tricolored twisted cord with lip
1 yard of 3"-wide rose-and-green tasseled decorative trim
21" x 15" pillow form

DIRECTIONS
All seams are ½".

1. Block needlepoint.

2. Trim canvas ½" from last row of stitches.

3. Cut two 22" x 16" pieces from velvet for pillow front and back.

4. Baste and sew design to the top of one piece of velvet, aligning the top edge of design with a long edge of fabric and centering it from side to side.

5. Baste and sew decorative trim to the sides of design next to stitching, covering raw canvas and mitering the trim at the point.

6. Baste and sew cording around sides and bottom edge of design unit, rounding corners slightly.

7. With right sides together, baste and sew pillow front and back together, leaving a 7" opening for turning.

8. Trim corners and turn right side out.

9. Insert pillow form into pillow. Slip-stitch opening closed.

Top Left Center

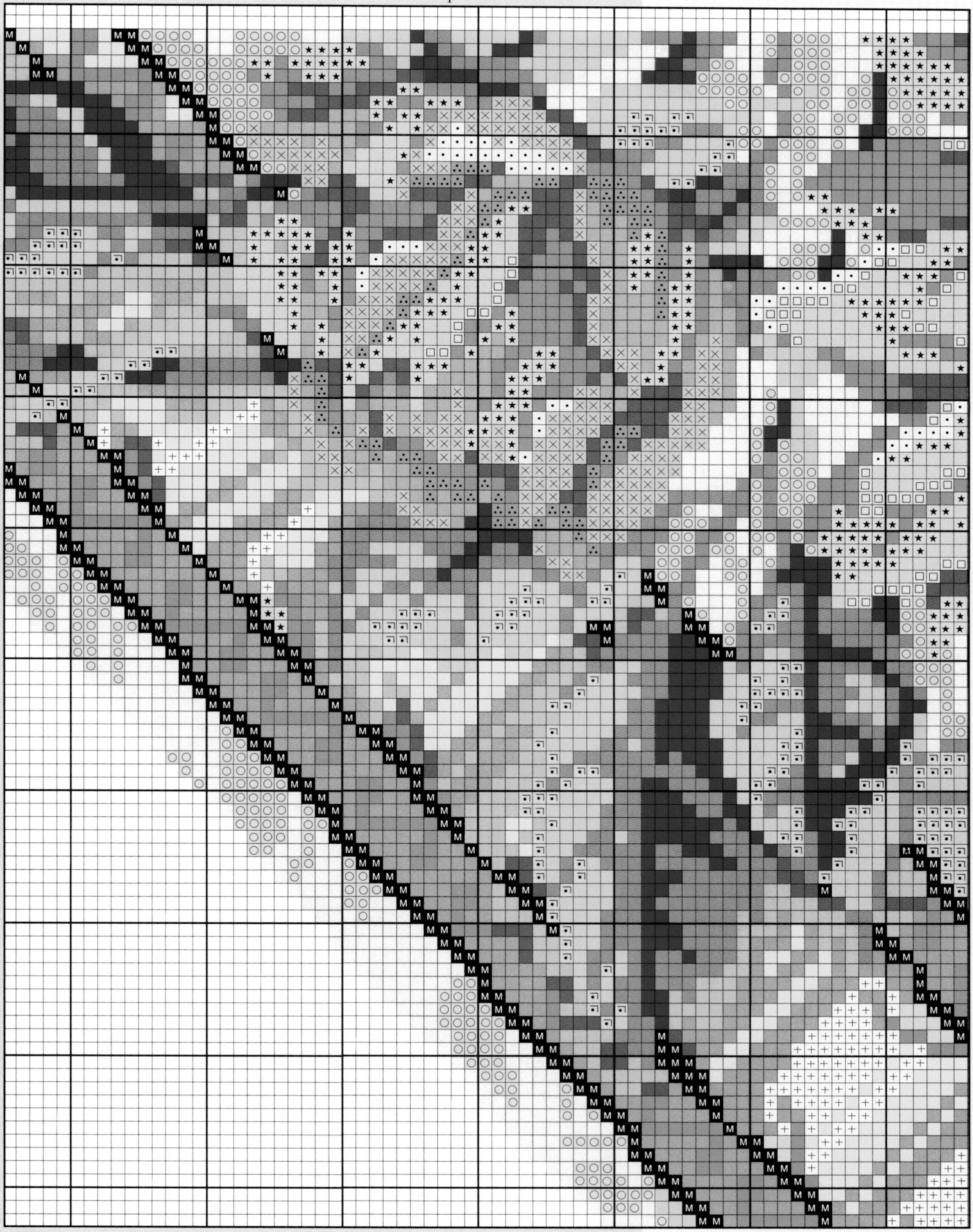

Top Right Center

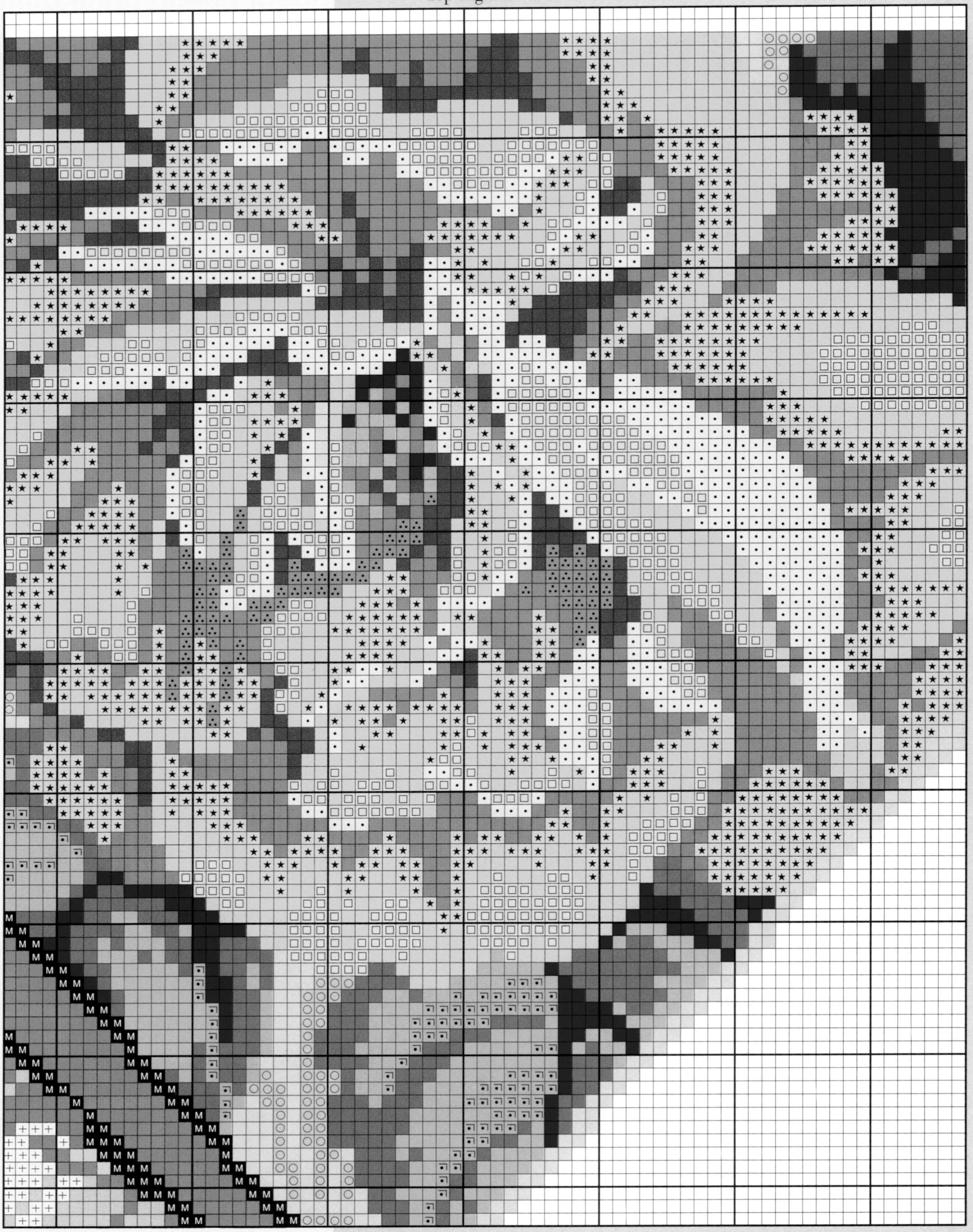

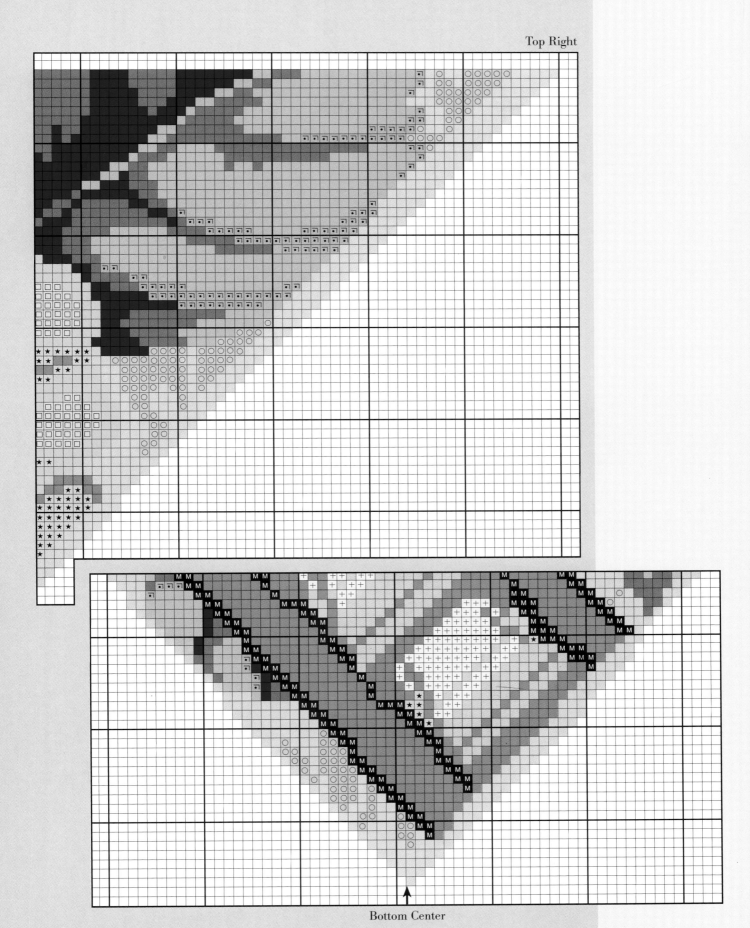

Golden Trout Pond

Stitched on 12-mesh canvas, the finished design size is 16½" x 12". The stitch count is 189 x 132. The canvas was cut 23" x 18".

Other Canvases	Design Sizes
10 count	18⅞" x 13¼"
13 count	14½" x 10⅛"
14 count	13½" x 9⅜"
18 count	10½" x 7⅞"

DMC		Paternayan Persian Yarn (used for sample)	

Step 1: Continental Stitch (2 ply)

DMC			Name
746	+	715	Mustard–vy. lt.
3822		727	Autumn Yellow–ultra vy. lt.
783		724	Autumn Yellow
3776	W	721	Autumn Yellow–vy. dk.
353	□	835	Bittersweet–vy.lt.
3341	∴	833	Bittersweet
225		935	Rusty Rose–vy. lt.
818	○	947	Cranberry–vy. lt.
3716		906	American Beauty–vy. lt.
962	★	904	American Beauty
3325	H	505	Federal Blue–lt.
3813		525	Teal Blue–vy. lt.
3817	△	523	Teal Blue
369	╱	614	Hunter Green–lt.
368	S	604	Forest Green–lt.
3815		662	Pine Green–med.
561		661	Pine Green–dk.
472	✕	654	Olive Green–lt.
3013		653	Olive Green
3012		652	Olive Green–med.
3011	♥	650	Olive Green–vy. dk.
310		220	Black

Step 2: Backstitch (1 ply)

310		220	Black

Top Left

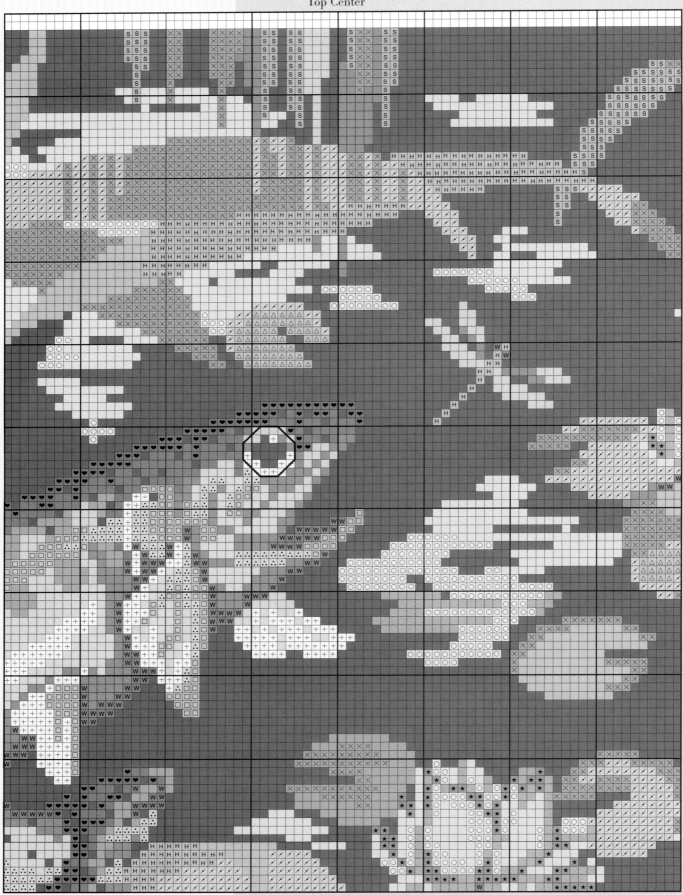

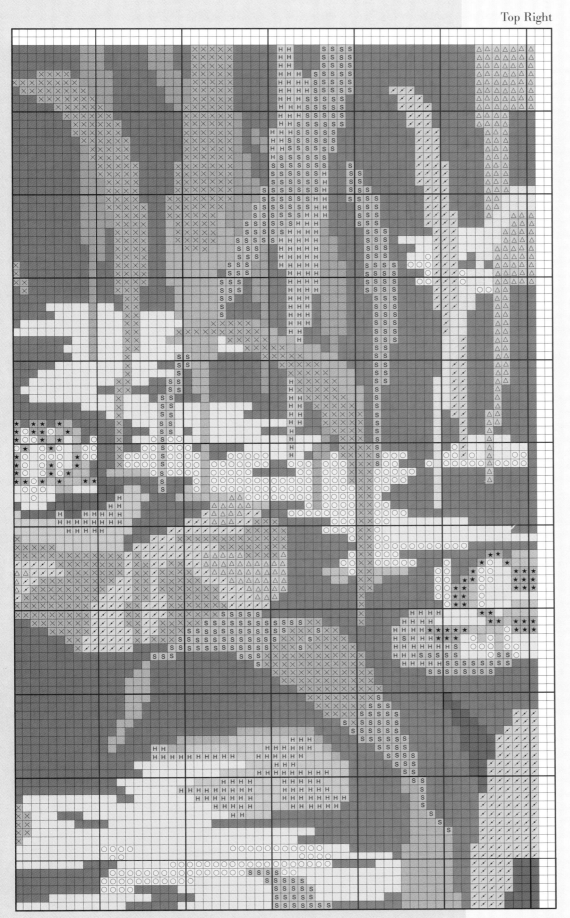

Footstool Finishing

MATERIALS

Completed design
on 12-mesh
canvas
Footstool with
design opening
of 15" x 10" and
muslin-covered
insert
1⅝ yards of ¼"-wide
dark teal green
twisted cord
with lip
Heavy-duty stapler
and ¼" staples
Screwdriver

DIRECTIONS

1. Block
needlepoint.

2. Baste and sew
cording around
edges of stitching,
overlapping ends
on one side.

3. Remove
muslin-covered
insert from
footstool.

4. Center design
unit over insert
and staple edges of
canvas to back,
mitering the
corners as needed.

*(Continued on
page 42)*

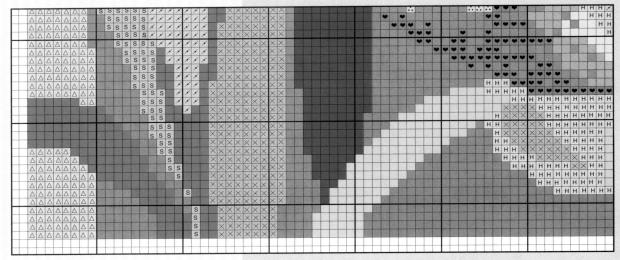

Bottom Left

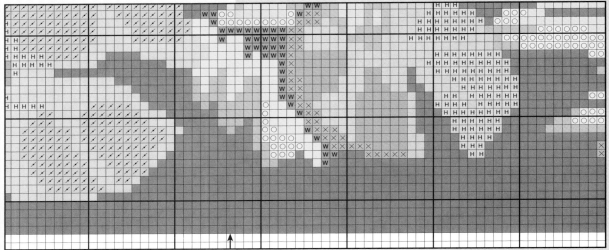

Bottom Center

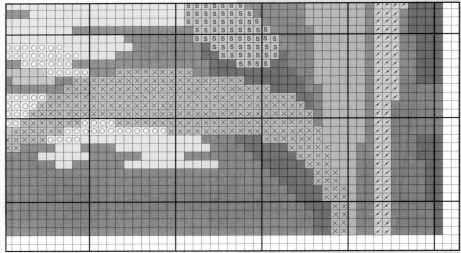

Bottom Right

(Continued from page 41)

5. Trim excess canvas from back of insert.

6. Replace insert in footstool and screw to secure in place.

Colonial Sampler

Stitched on 12-mesh canvas, the finished design size is 15" x 15". The stitch count is 173 x 173. The canvas was cut 21" x 21".

OTHER CANVASES	DESIGN SIZES
10 count	17¼" x 17¼"
13 count	13¼" x 13¼"
14 count	12⅜" x 12⅜"
18 count	9⅝" x 9⅝"

DMC		Paternayan Persian Yarn (used for sample)

Step 1: Continental Stitch (2 ply)

DMC		Persian	Color
712		261	Off White
3822	+	727	Autumn Yellow–ultra vy. lt.
783		724	Autumn Yellow
352		863	Copper
3687		910	Dusty Pink–vy. dk.
3325		504	Federal Blue
334	★	503	Federal Blue–med.
322		502	Federal Blue–dk.
3346		612	Hunter Green–med.
501		521	Teal Blue–dk.
841		463	Beige Brown–lt.
839		461	Beige Brown–med.

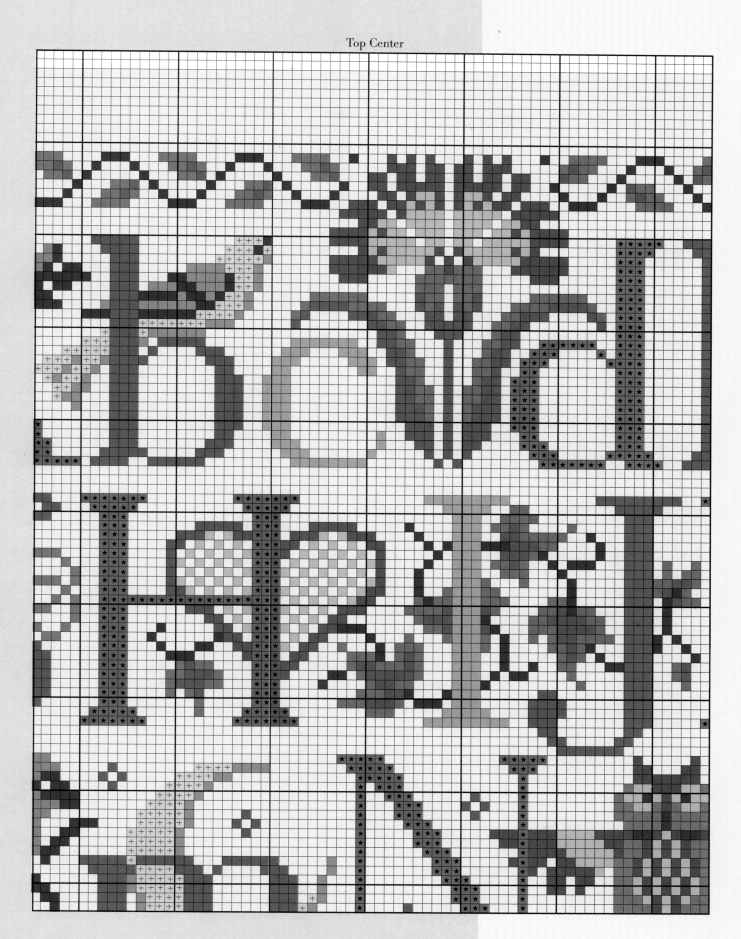

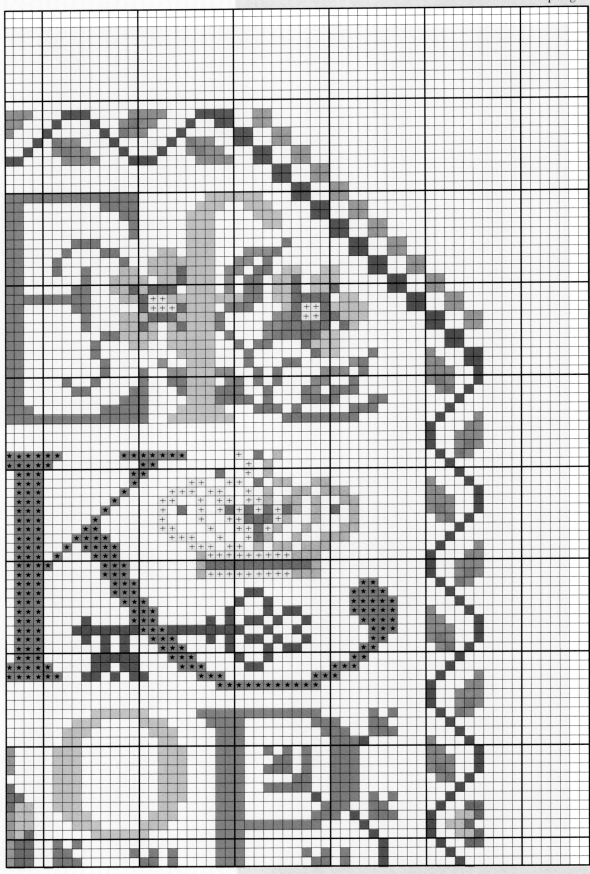

Bottom Left

Bottom Center

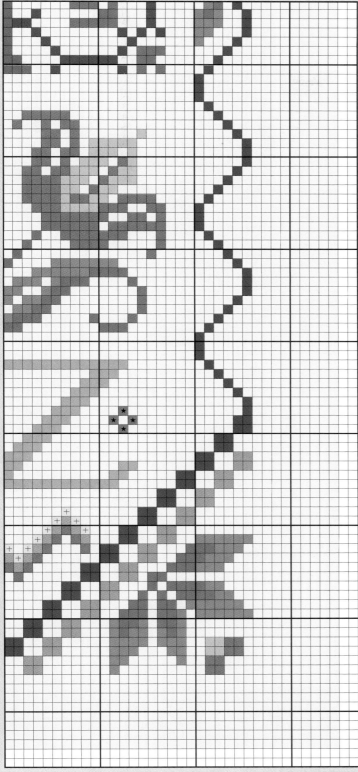

Bottom Right

Colonial Alphabet

See photo on page 50. Stitched on 18-mesh canvas, the finished design size is 37" x 3". The stitch count is 661 x 49. The canvas was cut 9" x 43". Graph begins on page 51. See "Draft Dodger Finishing" instructions below.

OTHER CANVASES	DESIGN SIZES
10 count	66⅛" x 4⅞"
12 count	55⅛" x 4⅛"
13 count	50⅞" x 3¾"
14 count	47¼" x 3½"

DMC		Paternayan Persian Yarn (used for sample)	
Step 1: Continental Stitch (1 ply)			
712		261	Off White
3822	+	727	Autumn Yellow–ultra vy. lt.
783		724	Autumn Yellow
352		863	Copper
3687		910	Dusty Pink–vy. dk.
3325		504	Federal Blue
334	★	503	Federal Blue–med.
322		502	Federal Blue–dk.
3346		612	Hunter Green–med.
501		521	Teal Blue–dk.
841		463	Beige Brown–lt.
839		461	Beige Brown–med.

Draft Dodger Finishing

MATERIALS

Completed design on 18-mesh canvas

⅓ yard of decorator-weight fabric; matching thread

2⅓ yards of ¼"-wide rose twisted cord with lip

37"-long piece of 3" equilateral triangular-shaped foam

(continued on page 50)

(continued from page 49)

DIRECTIONS
All seams are ½".

1. Block needlepoint.

2. Baste and sew cording around edges of stitching, overlapping ends on a short side and rounding corners slightly.

3. Trim canvas even with tape on cording.

4. Using design fabric as pattern, cut two pieces from decorator fabric.

5. With right sides together, baste and sew a fabric piece to each long edge of the design.

6. With right sides together, baste and sew remaining long edge of decorator fabrics together, leaving a 12" opening for turning.

7. Using Triangle Pattern on page 60, cut two pieces of decorator fabric for ends.

8. With rights sides together, baste and sew end pieces to design unit, aligning points with the seams.

9. Trim corners and turn right side out.

10. Stuff firmly, retaining triangular shape. Slip-stitch opening closed.

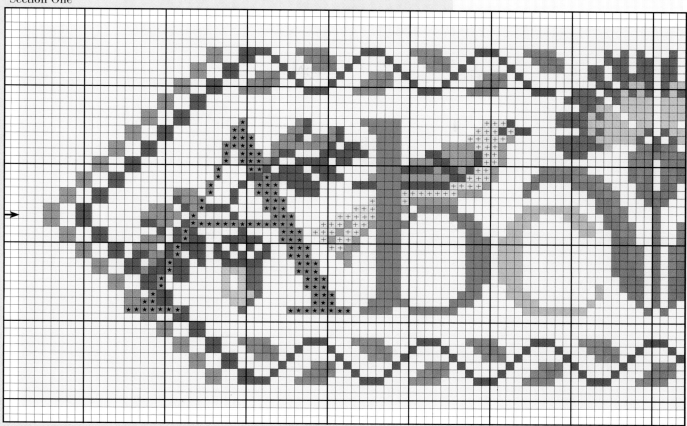

Section Two

Section Three

Section Four

Section Five

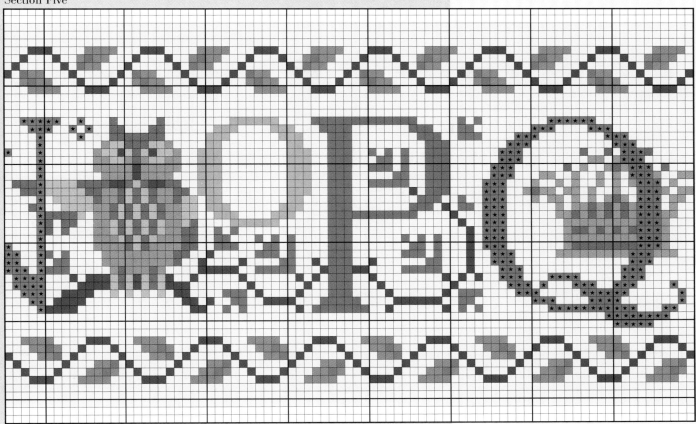

Section Six

Section Seven

Section Eight

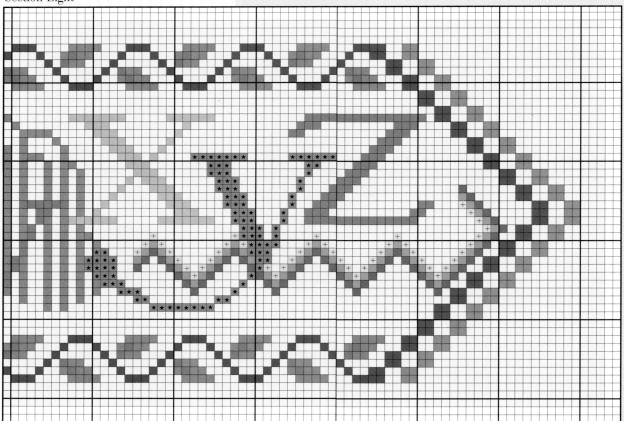

Summer Concerto

Stitched on 12-mesh canvas, the finished design size is 16⅛" x 12⅛". The stitch count is 193 x 145. The canvas was cut 23" x 19".

OTHER CANVASES	DESIGN SIZES
10 count	19¼" x 14½"
13 count	14⅞" x 11⅛"
14 count	13¾" x 10⅜"
18 count	10¾" x 8⅛"

DMC		Paternayan Persian Yarn (used for sample)	

Step 1: Continental Stitch (2 ply)

White	·	260	White
746	+	715	Mustard–vy. lt.
3822	○	727	Autumn Yellow–ultra vy. lt.
754		865	Copper–vy. lt.
3340		844	Salmon–lt.
351	E	843	Salmon
778		915	Dusty Pink–vy. lt.
604	△	905	American Beauty–lt.
601		903	American Beauty–med.
814		901	American Beauty–vy. dk.
321	N	969	Christmas Red–dk.
3743	⊠	334	Lavender–vy. lt.
209		313	Grape–med.
3747		344	Periwinkle–vy. lt.
341		343	Periwinkle–lt.
792		341	Periwinkle–med.
311		571	Navy Blue
772		635	Spring Green–vy. lt.
704		698	Christmas Green–lt.
988	□	612	Hunter Green–med.
987		611	Hunter Green–dk.
986		690	Loden Green–vy. dk.
951	H	805	Marigold–vy. lt.
437	∵	497	Wicker Brown
435		496	Wicker Brown–med.
402	S	855	Spice–vy. lt.
922	✎	884	Ginger–lt.
920	⊡	862	Copper–med.
919		860	Copper–vy. dk.
300	K	480	Terra Cotta–ultra vy. lt.
842		473	Toast Brown
840		472	Toast Brown–med.
839	♡	461	Beige Brown–med.
3371	⬚	421	Coffee Brown–med.
318		211	Pearl Gray
310	★	220	Black

56

Top Left

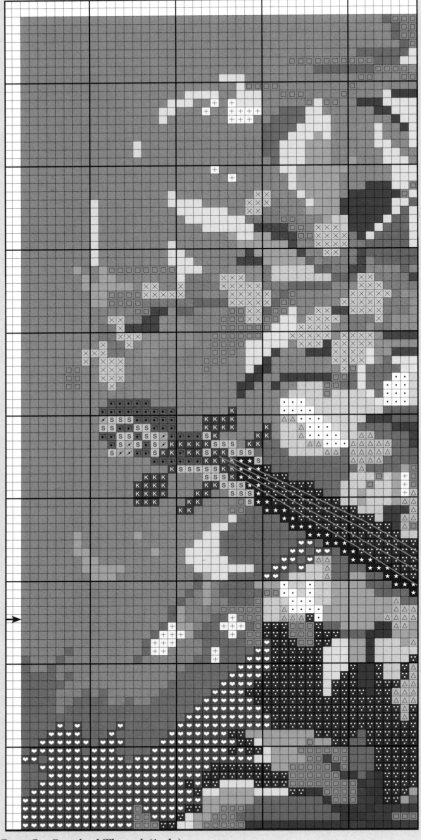

Step 2: Couched Thread (1 ply)

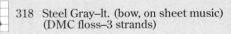

988	╲	612	Hunter Green–med.	318	╲	318	Steel Gray–lt. (bow, on sheet music) (DMC floss–3 strands)

318  318 Steel Gray–lt. (strings)
(DMC floss–1 strand)

317  317 Pewter Gray
(DMC floss–2 strands)

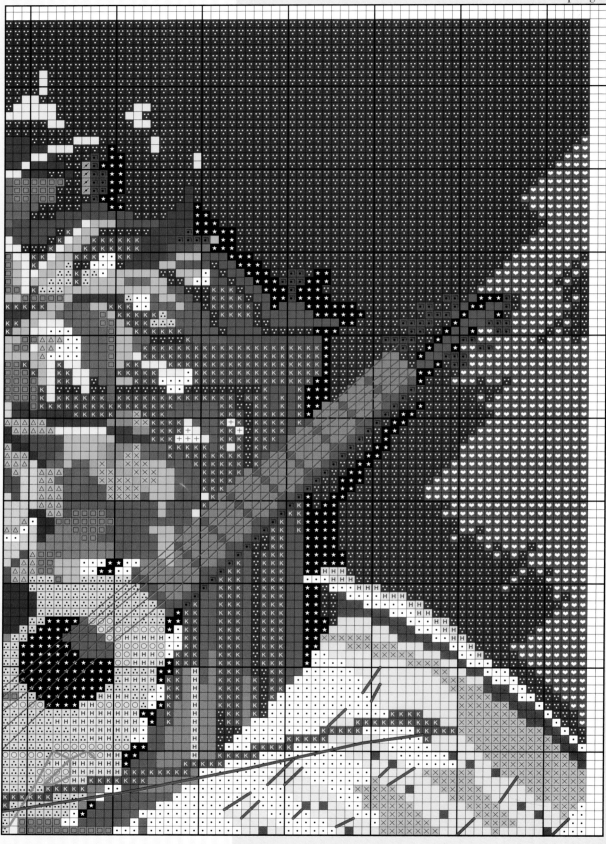

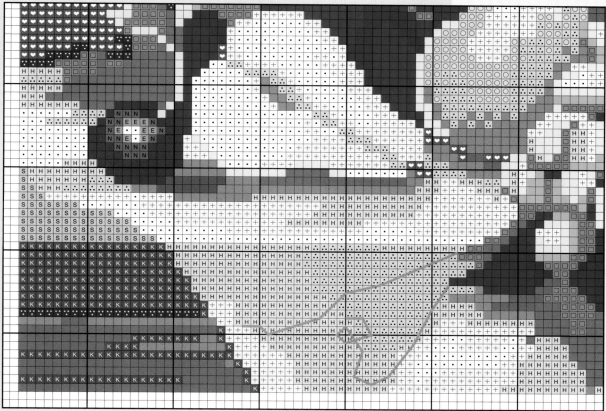

Bottom Left

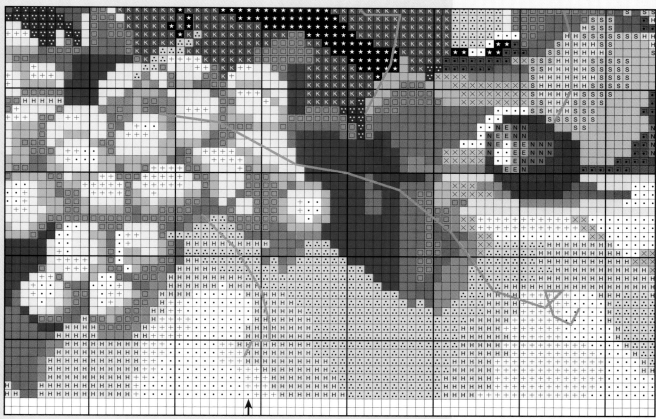

Bottom Center

59

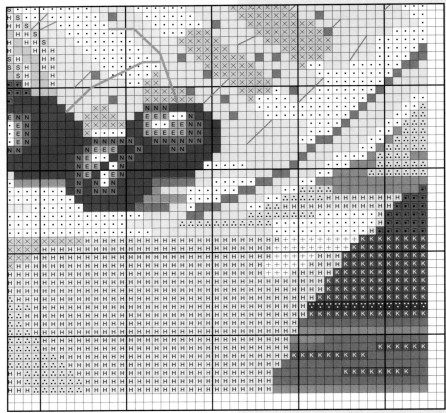

Bottom Right

Table Runner

Here's an extra idea. Isolate the fruits on the lower left of the design, from the cherry to the grape leaf motif, and cross-stitch, centering horizontally from both long edges and 2½" up from bottom short edge of a 15" x 47" piece of amaretto Murano 30 over two threads.

MATERIALS

Completed design
Matching thread

DIRECTIONS

1. Turn long edges under ¼" twice and slip-stitch for a ½" hem.

2. Turn short edges under ¼". Turn edges under ¾" again and slip-stitch for a 1" hem.

Hot Pad

Here's another idea. Isolate the cherry and pear motif in the lower left of the design, and cross-stitch in the center of a 6" square of amaretto Murano 30 over two threads.

MATERIALS

Completed design
8½" square of contrasting fabric; matching thread
Two 6" squares of fleece

DIRECTIONS

Layer fabrics as follows: contrasting fabric with wrong side up, two layers of fleece, and completed design fabric with right side up. Starting at bottom edge, roll hem up over edges and slip-stitch all around hot pad.

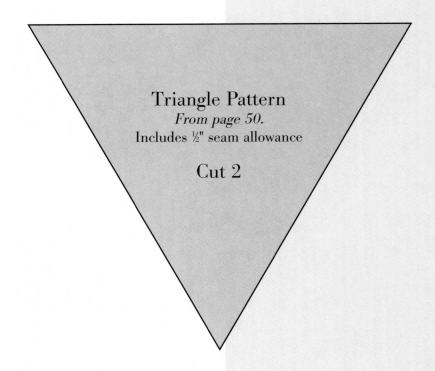

Triangle Pattern
From page 50.
Includes ½" seam allowance

Cut 2

Vintage Vines

Bench Cover

Stitched on 10-mesh canvas, the finished design size is 18¾" x 15". The stitch count is 189 x 143. The canvas was cut 25" x 21".

OTHER CANVASES	DESIGN SIZES
12 count	15¾" x 11⅞"
13 count	14½" x 11"
14 count	13½" x 10¼"
18 count	10½" x 8"

DMC		Paternayan Persian Yarn (used for sample)	

Step 1: Continental Stitch (2 ply)

3823		755	Old Gold–vy. lt.
676		734	Honey Gold–lt.
211		314	Grape–vy. lt.
208		312	Grape
550		311	Grape–med.
3740		320	Plum–ultra vy. dk.
3348		694	Loden Green–lt.
988		612	Hunter Green–med.
731		641	Khaki Green–dk.
3817		579	Turquoise–vy. lt.
562		663	Pine Green
500		660	Pine Green–vy. dk.
436	+	413	Earth Brown–lt.
434		412	Earth Brown

Step 2: Backstitch (2 ply)

988		612	Hunter Green–med. (vines)
434		412	Earth Brown (stems)

Top Left

Bench Cover Finishing

MATERIALS

Completed design on 10-mesh
    canvas
Footstool with design opening of
    17" x 13" and muslin-covered
    insert
Heavy-duty stapler and ¼" staples
Screwdriver

DIRECTIONS

1. Block needlepoint.

2. Remove muslin-covered
insert from footstool.

3. Center design unit over
insert and staple edges of canvas
to back, mitering the corners as
needed.

4. Trim excess canvas from
back of insert.

5. Replace insert in footstool,
and screw to secure in place.

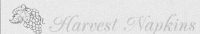 *Harvest Napkins*

Here's an extra idea. Isolate a
grape cluster and leaf motif, and
cross-stitch 1¼" in from both
edges of one corner on a 15"
square of ivory Murano 30 over
two threads.

MATERIALS (for one napkin)

Completed design

DIRECTIONS

1. Sew a narrow zigzag stitch ½"
from raw edge all around
completed design fabric.

2. Pull outer threads to zigzag
stitch to fray edges of napkin.

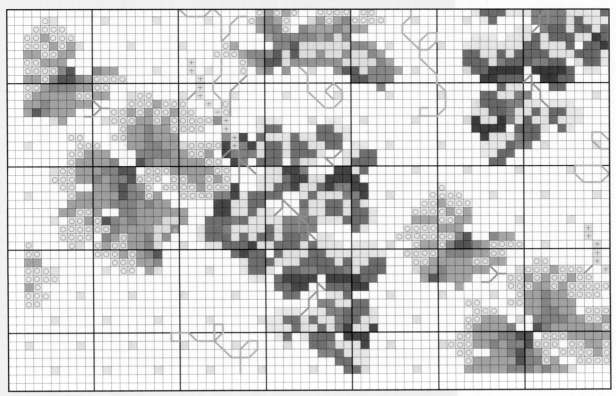

Bottom Left

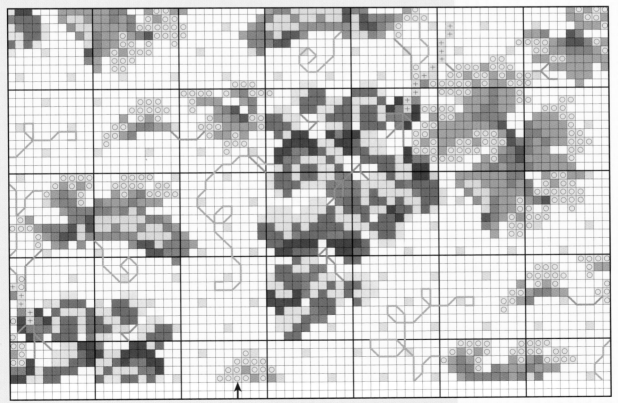

Bottom Center

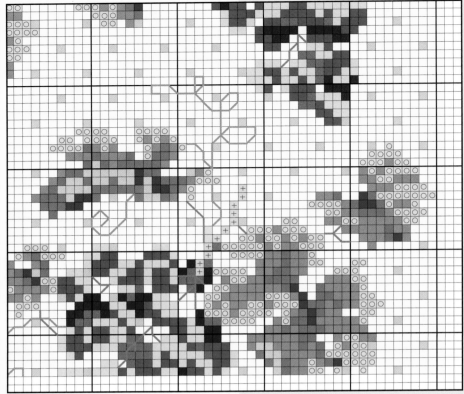

Bottom Right

Eyeglass Case

Stitched on 18-mesh canvas, the finished design size is 3½" x 7¼". The stitch count is 63 x 126. The canvas was cut 10" x 15". See "Eyeglass Case Finishing" for instructions on page 83.

OTHER CANVASES	DESIGN SIZES
10 count	6¼" x 12⅝"
12 count	5¼" x 10½"
13 count	4⅞" x 9¾"
14 count	4½" x 9"

Yarn		DMC (used for sample)	

Step 1: Continental Stitch (6 strands)

734		677	Old Gold–vy. lt.
314		210	Lavender–med.
312		553	Violet–med.
311		552	Violet–dk.
320		550	Violet–vy.dk.
694	○	3348	Yellow Green–lt.
612		3346	Hunter Green
641		730	Olive Green–vy. dk.
579		504	Blue Green–lt.
663		502	Blue Green
660		890	Pistachio Green–ultra dk.
755		738	Tan–vy. lt.
413	+	435	Brown–vy. lt.
412		433	Brown–med.

Step 2: Backstitch (3 strands)

612		3346	Hunter Green
412		433	Brown–med.

Top

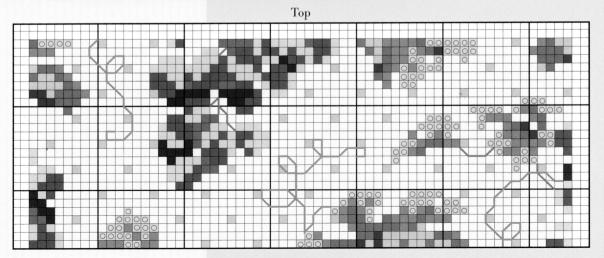

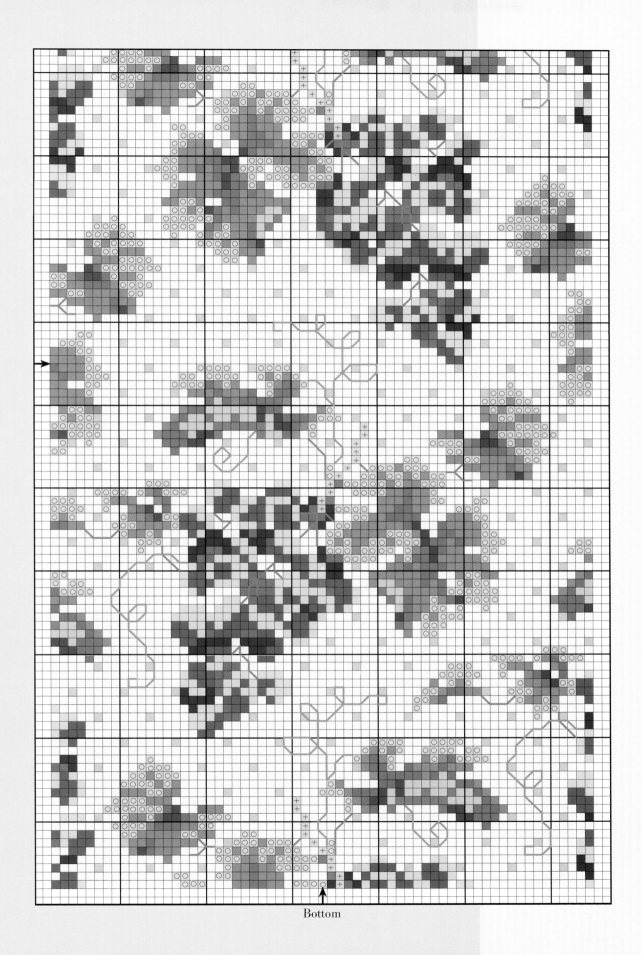

Bottom

Bountiful Harvest

Stitched on 12-mesh canvas, the finished design size is 19" x 10½". The stitch count is 231 x 124. The canvas was cut 25" x 17".

OTHER CANVASES	DESIGN SIZES
10 count	23⅛" x 12⅜"
13 count	17¾" x 9½"
14 count	16½" x 8⅞"
18 count	12⅞" x 6⅞"

DMC   Paternayan Persian Yarn (used for sample)

Step 1: Continental Stitch (2 ply)

DMC		Paternayan	
746	□	715	Mustard-vy. lt.
745	✓	704	Butterscotch-vy. lt.
743		815	Sunrise-vy. lt.
741		802	Marigold-med.
721		800	Marigold-vy. dk.
3341		833	Bittersweet
351	Z	843	Salmon
891		972	Christmas Red-lt.
666	U	970	Christmas Red-med.
304		968	Christmas Red-vy. dk.
221	H	920	Wood Rose-vy. dk.
341		343	Periwinkle-lt.

DMC		Paternayan	
333	N	340	Periwinkle-dk.
554		302	Violet
208		312	Grape
550		311	Grape-med.
3740		320	Plum-ultra vy. dk.
3807	★	560	Glacier-dk.
311	K	571	Navy Blue
813	○	553	Ice Blue
825		551	Ice Blue-dk.
369	×	615	Hunter Green-vy. lt.
3348		624	Shamrock-vy. lt.
955	△	623	Shamrock-lt.
772	•	695	Loden Green-vy. lt.
3347		693	Loden Green

Top Left

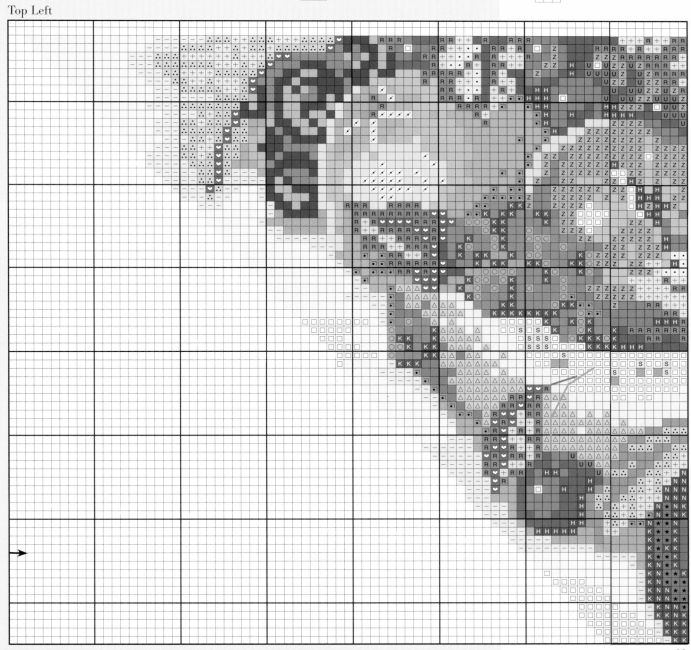

905		696	Christmas Green-med.
469	E	651	Olive Green-dk.
522		600	Forest Green-vy. dk.
598	∴	522	Teal Blue-med.
501		521	Teal Blue-dk.
504	+	664	Pine Green-lt.
562		663	Pine Green
3815	R	662	Pine Green-med.
561	♥	661	Pine Green-dk.
500		660	Pine Green-vy. dk.
739		499	Wicker Brown-vy. lk.
738	–	498	Wicker Brown-lt.
437	S	497	Wicker Brown
435		496	Wicker Brown-med.

| 420 | ⊡ | 424 | Coffee Brown-vy. lt. |
| 841 | | 463 | Beige Brown-lt. |

Step 2: Couched Yarn (1 ply)

| 420 | | 424 | Coffee Brown-vy. lt. |
| 561 | | 661 | Pine Green–dk. |

MATERIALS

Completed design on 12-mesh canvas

½ yard of purple velvet upholstery-weight fabric; matching thread

1 yard of ½"-wide flat purple-and-green decorative trim

1½ yards of 3½"-wide scalloped-edge purple-and-green tasseled decorative trim

21" x 14" pillow form

Top Center

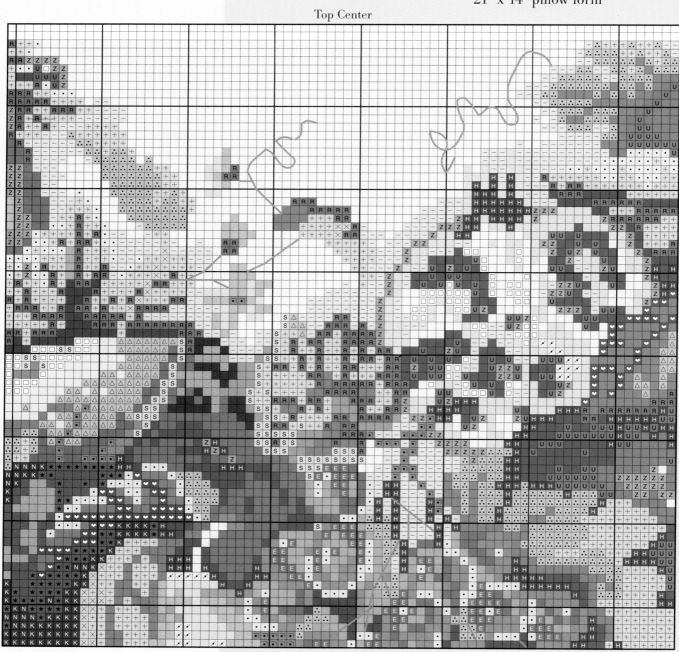

DIRECTIONS
All seams are ½".

1. Block needlepoint.

2. Trim canvas ½" from last row of stitches.

3. Cut two 22" x 15" pieces from velvet for pillow front and back.

4. Baste and sew design to the top of one piece of velvet, aligning the top edge of design with a long edge of fabric and centering it from side to side.

5. Baste and sew flat decorative trim to the sides of design next to stitching, covering raw canvas and mitering the trim at the point, if needed.

6. Baste and sew wide decorative trim to the sides and bottom of design unit only, positioning flat edge of trim approximately 1½" in from edge of fabric, and rounding corners slightly.

7. With right sides together, baste and sew pillow front and back together, taking care to keep tassels out of seam and leaving a 7" opening for turning.

8. Trim corners and turn right side out. Insert pillow form into pillow. Slip-stitch opening closed.

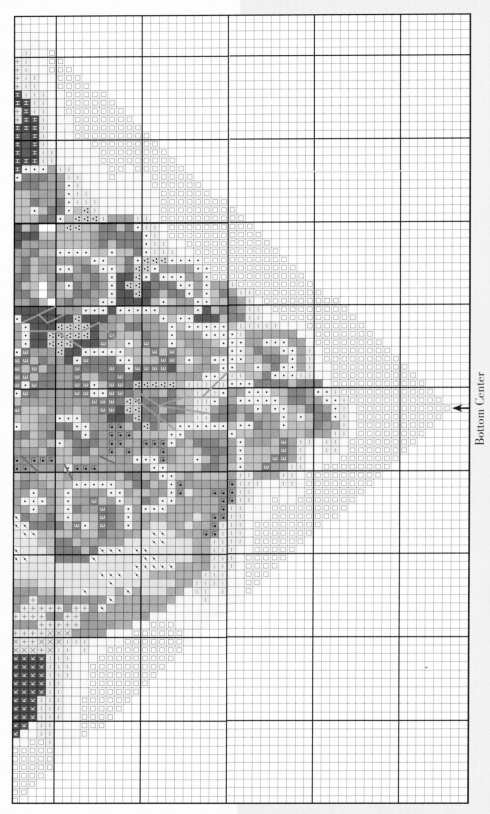

Here's an extra idea. For a decorative tassel, wrap floss or ribbon around a 2" x 3" cardboard piece to make a thick bundle (see Diagram A). Thread needle with a length of same color of floss. Slide needle under one end of bundle (see Diagram B). Pull needle free and tie floss in very tight knot around bundle. Cut bundle at end opposite knot (see Diagram C). Wrap separate length of floss several times around bundle and knot to secure (see Diagram D). Trim ends of tassel even.

Bottom Center

Diagram A

Diagram B

Diagram C

Diagram D

Golden Tassels

Stitched on 12-mesh canvas, the finished design size is 14⅛" x 11⅛". The stitch count is 167 x 131. The canvas was cut 20" x 17".

OTHER CANVASES	DESIGN SIZES
10 count	16¾" x 13⅛"
13 count	12⅞" x 10⅛"
14 count	11⅞" x 9⅜"
18 count	9¼" x 7¼"

DMC   Paternayan Persian Yarn (used for sample)

Step 1: Continental Stitch (2 ply)

DMC		Paternayan	
814	N	901	American Beauty–vy. dk.
327		321	Plum–vy. dk.
333	★	331	Lavender–med.
798		541	Cobalt Blue–dk.
796	R	540	Cobalt Blue–vy. dk.
311	♥	571	Navy Blue
3363		603	Forest Green
469		651	Olive Green–dk.
561	E	661	Pine Green–dk.
780		495	Wicker Brown–dk.
919		860	Copper–vy. dk.
300	+	400	Fawn Brown–vy. dk.
839	W	461	Beige Brown–med.
898		431	Chocolate Brown–vy. dk.
3078		3078	Golden Yellow–vy. lt. (DMC floss–6 strands)
676		676	Old Gold–lt. (DMC floss–6 strands)
783		783	Christmas Gold (DMC floss–6 strands)
721		721	Orange Spice–med. (DMC floss–6 strands)
921	×	921	Copper (DMC floss–6 strands)
666	H	666	Christmas Red–bright (DMC floss–6 strands)
420		420	Hazel Nut Brown–dk. (DMC floss–6 strands)
869	K	869	Hazel Nut Brown–vy. dk. (DMC floss–6 strands)

Top Left

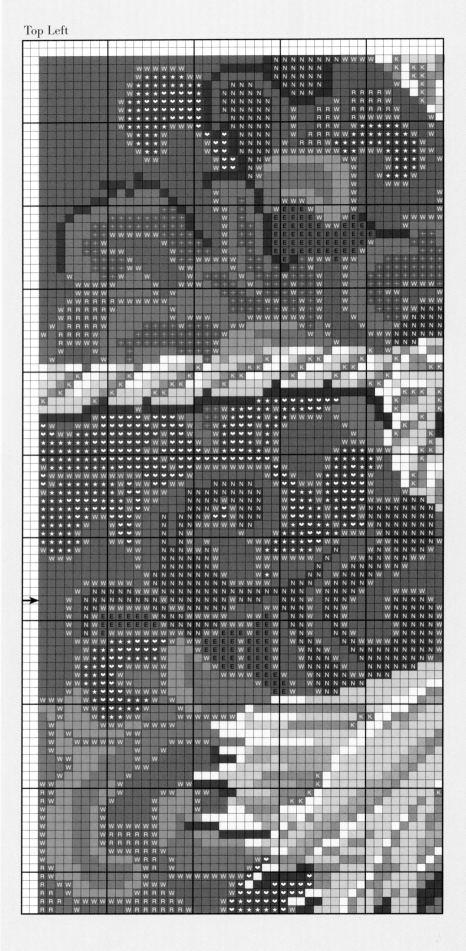

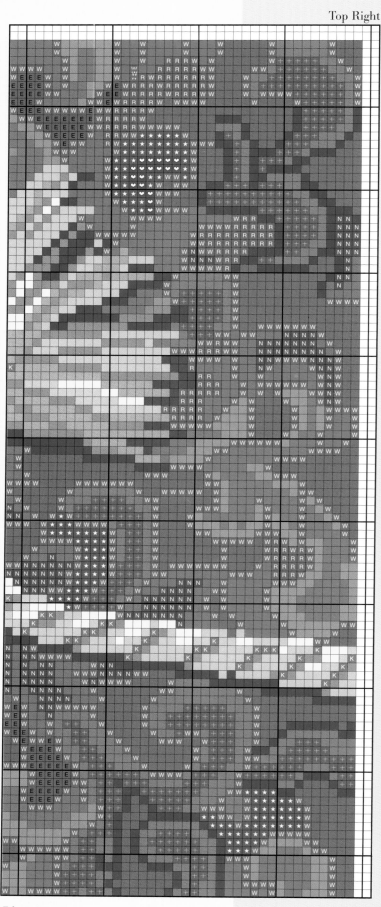

MATERIALS

Completed design on 12-mesh canvas
⅔ yard of purple velvet upholstery-weight
    fabric; matching thread
3 yards of ¾"-wide cord for tubing
11" x 14" pillow form

DIRECTIONS
All seams are ½".

1. Make tubing for pillow edge by cutting a 2" x 60" strip of velvet. With wrong sides together, fold in half lengthwise. Sew a seam down this long edge. Thread cord through tubing. Repeat for other seamed pillow edge.

2. Block needlepoint.

3. Trim canvas ½" from last row of stitches.

4. Using design as pattern, cut one piece from velvet for pillow back.

5. Cut a 51" x 4" strip from velvet for pillow sides.

6. With right sides together, place and pin the first tubing (raw edges together) and then the side strip to design fabric. Baste around design along last row of stitches.

7. Baste side strip ends together. Trim any excess fabric.

8. With right sides together, baste pillow back and remaining edge of side strip, leaving a 6" opening for turning.

9. Trim corners and turn right side out.

10. Insert pillow form into pillow. Slip-stitch opening closed.

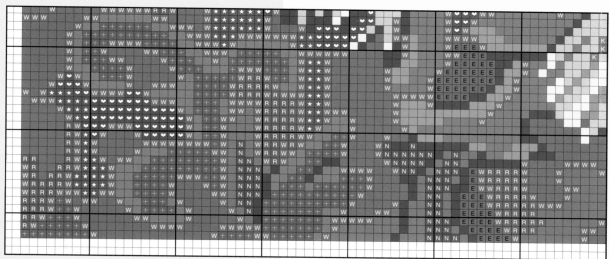

Bottom Left

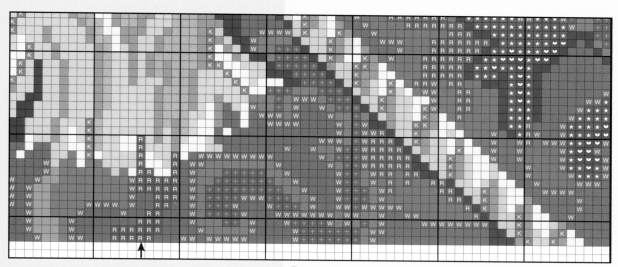

Bottom Center

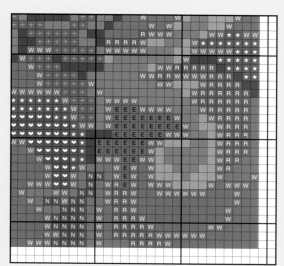

Bottom Right

More Golden Ideas

Customize the Golden Tassels piece by using some of the following techniques:

1. Work the "cord" and "tassels" on the design in a different fiber that has a lustrous quality such as Marlitt or pearl cotton. This adds sheen and dimension to the piece.

2. Replace the tubing/piping with cording made from the same fibers as used to work the "cord" of the "tassels" on the design. The cording will appear to continue from the design and surround the pillow. See "Making Cording" directions on page 90.

3. Add seed beads to the orange and gold areas of the heads of the "tassels" to create dimension.

Lotsa Puppies

Stitched on 12-mesh canvas,
the finished design size is 16⅛" x
11⅞". The stitch count is 193 x
142. The canvas was cut 23" x 18".

Other Canvases	Design Sizes
10 count	19¼" x 14¼"
13 count	14⅞" x 10⅞"
14 count	13¾" x 10⅛"
18 count	10¾" x 7⅞"

DMC | **Paternayan Persian Yarn (used for sample)**

Step 1: Continental Stitch (2 ply)

DMC		Paternayan	
White	·	260	White
Ecru	+	262	Ecru
951		805	Marigold–vy. lt.
945	○	824	Tangerine–lt.
743		815	Sunrise–vy. lt.
963	–	946	Cranberry–lt.
3708	s	944	Cranberry–med.
335		942	Cranberry–vy. dk.
326		940	Cranberry–deep
3806		962	Hot Pink
775		546	Cobalt Blue–ultra vy. lt.
827	∴	554	Ice Blue–lt.
334		503	Federal Blue–med.
3750		501	Federal Blue–vy. dk.
959		593	Caribbean Blue
564	□	577	Turquoise
563	N	575	Turquoise–dk.
562		574	Turquoise–vy. dk.
561		661	Pine Green–dk.
772		695	Loden Green–vy. lt.
3013		653	Olive Green
988		612	Hunter Green–med.
3826	E	883	Ginger
920	✷	882	Ginger–med.
543	△	475	Toast Brown–vy. lt.
842		473	Toast Brown
434		412	Earth Brown
300		400	Fawn Brown–vy. dk.
898	H	431	Chocolate Brown–vy. dk.
3747	×	344	Periwinkle–vy. lt.
318		211	Pearl Gray
310	♥	220	Black

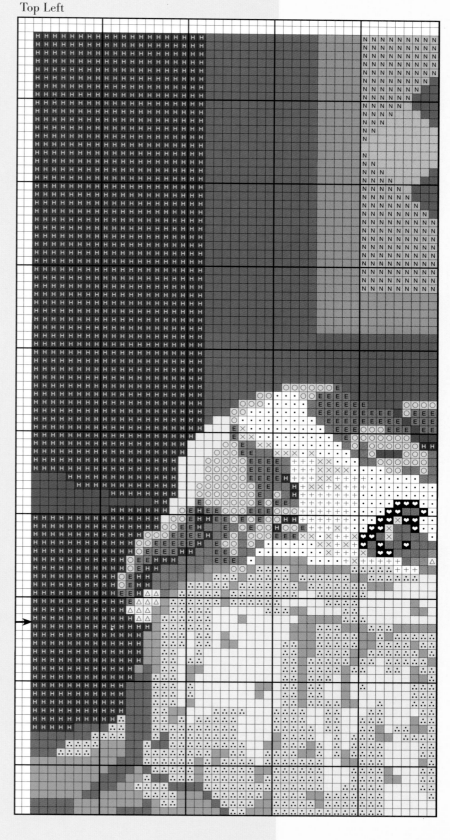

Top Left

Step 2: Backstitch (1 ply)

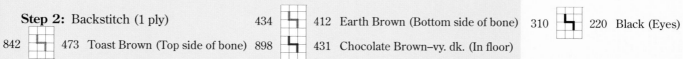

842 | 473 Toast Brown (Top side of bone)
434 | 412 Earth Brown (Bottom side of bone)
898 | 431 Chocolate Brown–vy. dk. (In floor)
310 | 220 Black (Eyes)

Top Center

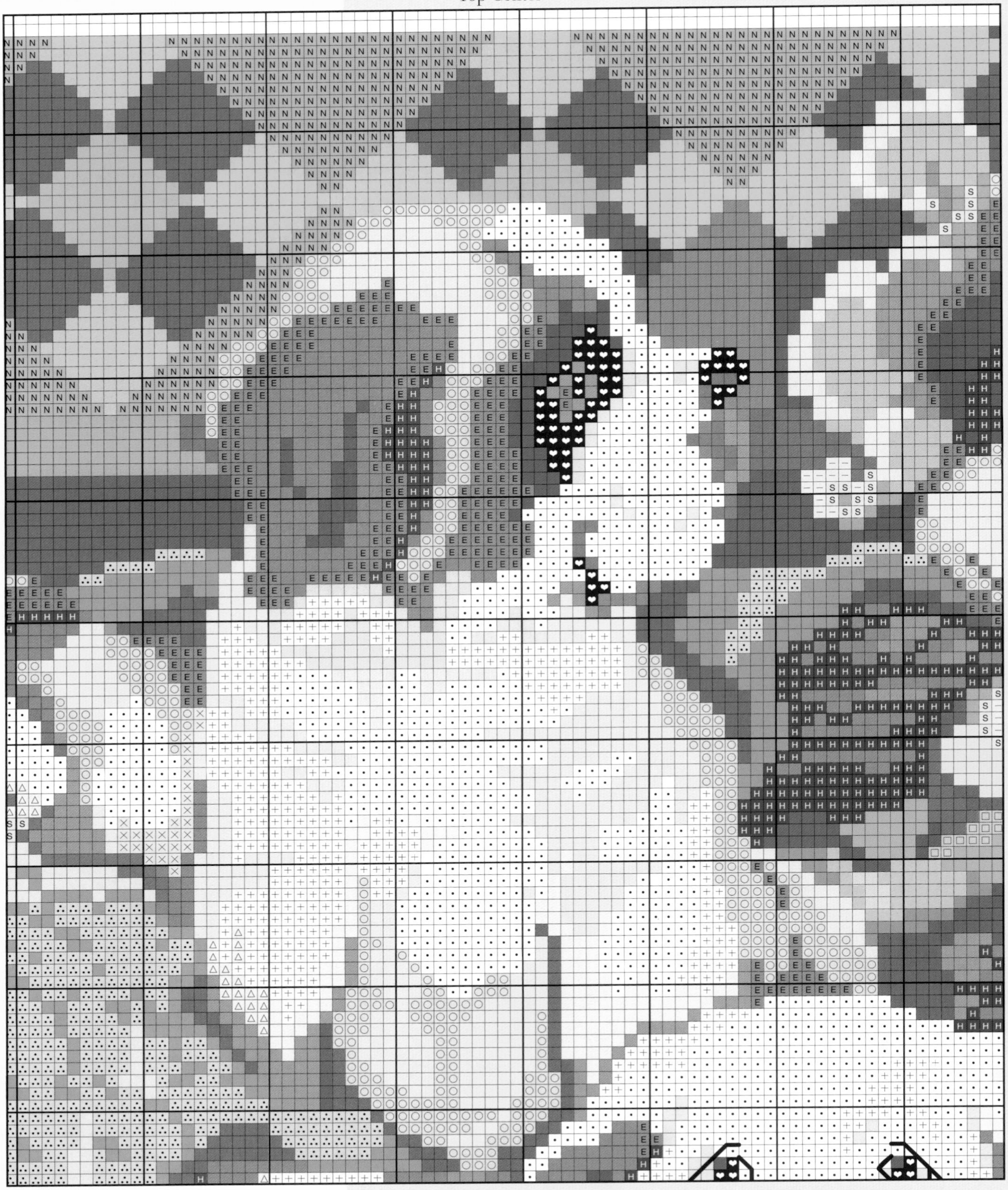

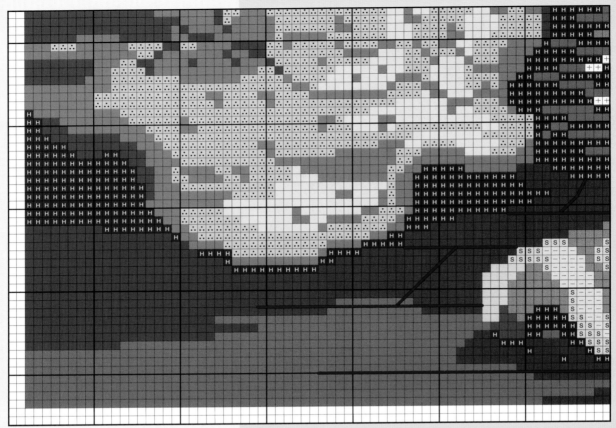

Bottom Left

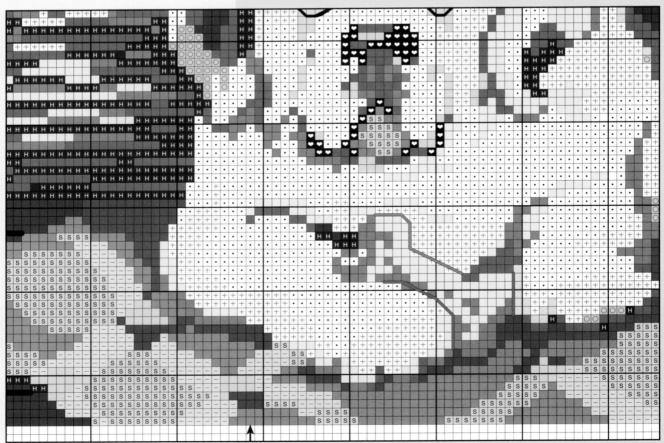

Bottom Center

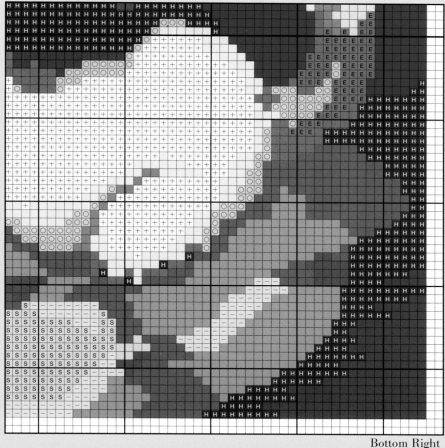

Bottom Right

Puppy Chest

Here's an extra idea. Place these puppies on the lid of a keepsake chest.

MATERIALS

Completed design on 12-mesh canvas
Chest with design opening of 16" x 11½" and muslin-covered insert
Heavy-duty stapler and ¼" staples
Screwdriver

DIRECTIONS

1. Block needlepoint.

2. Remove muslin-covered insert from chest lid.

3. Center completed design over insert, and staple edges of canvas to back, mitering the corners as needed.

4. Trim excess canvas from back of insert.

5. Replace insert in chest lid and screw to secure in place.

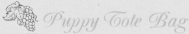

Puppy Tote Bag

Here's another idea. Create a tote for carrying all the needed accessories for today's person or puppy on the go.

On a purchased tote bag, center a 13" x 8" piece of Waste Canvas 14. Isolate the puppy and pink blanket motif in the lower right foreground of the design and cross-stitch.

Eyeglass Case Finishing
From page 66.

MATERIALS

Completed design on 18-mesh canvas
¼ yard of purple satin; matching thread
¼ yard of purple velvet
⅝ yard of ⅛"-diameter purple rat-tail cording

DIRECTIONS
All seams are ½".

1. Block needlepoint.

2. Trim canvas ½" from last row of stitches.

3. Using design canvas as pattern, cut two pieces of satin and one piece of velvet fabric for case lining and back.

4. With right sides together, baste and sew velvet piece to the design, leaving the top edge open. Clip corners and turn right side out.

5. Using sewing thread, tack rat-tail cording to case along seam lines.

6. With right sides together, baste and sew satin pieces together, leaving the top edge and 3" of a long seam open. Clip corners.

7. With right sides together, baste and sew top edge of case and lining together. Turn right side out.

8. Slip-stitch opening in lining closed and insert it in case.

Kriss Kringle

Stitched on 12-mesh canvas, the finished design size is 9¾" x 16⅜". The stitch count is 112 x 196. The canvas was cut 14" x 21".

OTHER CANVASES	DESIGN SIZES
10 count	11½" x 19⅝"
13 count	8⅞" x 15⅛"
14 count	8¼" x 14"
18 count	6⅜" x 10⅞"

DMC — Paternayan Persian Yarn (used for sample)

Step 1: Continental Stitch (2 ply)

DMC		Paternayan	
White	·	260	White
745		704	Butterscotch–vy. lt.
725		702	Butterscotch
782	×	701	Butterscotch–med.
781	N	700	Butterscotch–dk.
3822	∴	727	Autumn Yellow–ultra vy. lt.
783		724	Autumn Yellow
977		723	Autumn Yellow-med.
3376	S	721	Autumn Yellow–vy. dk.
754	–	490	Flesh–dk.
761		934	Rusty Rose–lt.
760	□	933	Rusty Rose
891	△	972	Christmas Red–lt.
666		970	Christmas Red–med.
347		968	Christmas Red–vy. dk.
902		900	American Beauty–ultra vy. dk.
554		302	Violet
553	∕	301	Violet–med.
552		300	Violet–dk.
799		543	Cobalt Blue
798	★	541	Cobalt Blue–dk.
796		540	Cobalt Blue–vy. dk.
959	E	593	Caribbean Blue
958	▼	592	Caribbean Blue–med.
702		621	Shamrock–med.
700	H	620	Shamrock–dk.
561		661	Pine Green–dk.
437	○	497	Wicker Brown
435		496	Wicker Brown–med.
762	+	237	Silver Gray
415		564	Glacier–vy. lt.
310	M	220	Black

Step 2: Backstitch (1 ply)

760		933	Rusty Rose (nose)
666		970	Christmas Red–med (lettering, mouth)
441		869	Hazel Nut Brown–vy. dk. (DMC 2 strands, eye)

Step 3: Long Loose Stitch (1 strand)

DMC Light Gold Thread (Fil or clair)

Step 4: Stars on Bag (3 strands)

DMC Light Gold Thread (Fil or clair)

Step 5: Couched Thread (2 strands)

DMC Light Gold Thread (Fil or clair)

Step 6: Stars and Bells

● Placement of stars and bells.

Stocking Finishing

MATERIALS

Completed design on 12-mesh canvas

½ yd. gold decorator-weight fabric; matching thread

Gold metallic cord-and-tassel tieback unit (cord approximately 28" with 3"-long tassels)

Two ⅝"-diameter gold tone star buttons

Two ¼"-diameter gold tone jingle bells

DIRECTIONS

All seams are ½".

1. Block needlepoint.

2. Trim canvas ½" from last row of stitches around stocking.

(continued on page 89)

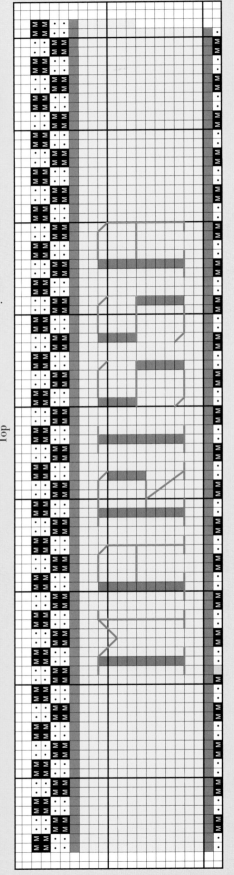

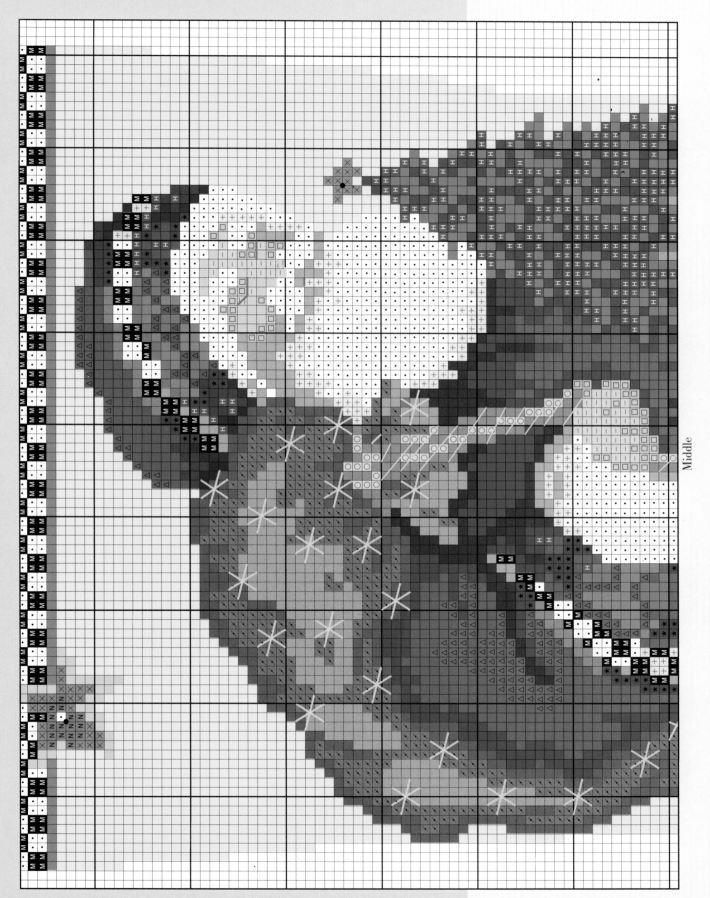

Middle

87

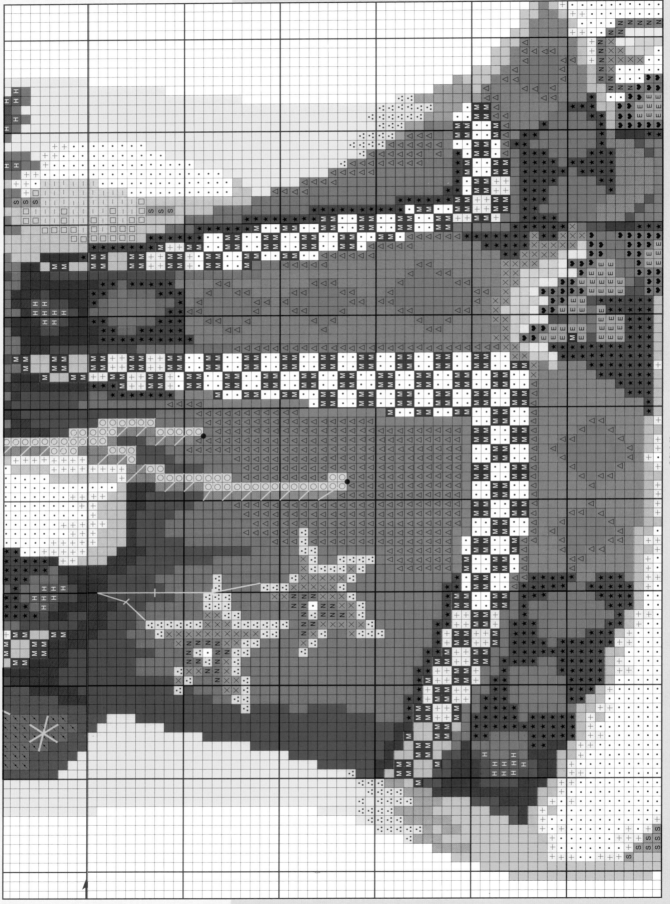

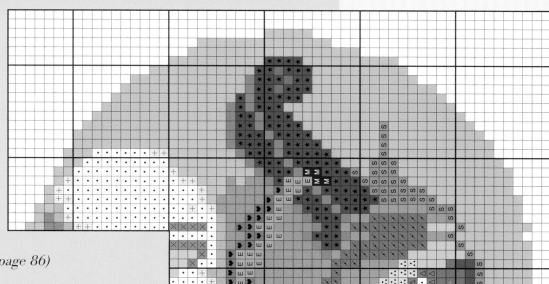

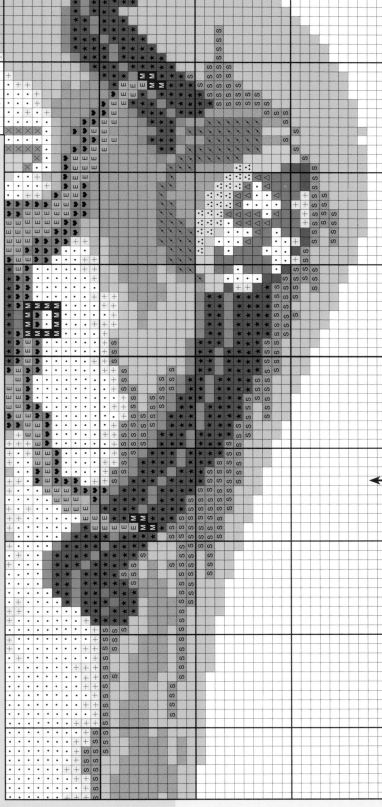

(continued from page 86)

3. Using design as pattern, cut three pieces of decorator fabric for stocking lining and back.

4. Sew a star button over the stitched star in the checkerboard border and at top of tree (refer to photo for placement).

5. Sew a bell to each end of stitched cord of top bag.

6. With right sides together, baste and sew one decorator fabric piece to the stocking, leaving the top edge open. Clip curves and turn right side out.

7. With right sides together, baste and sew remaining fabric pieces together, leaving the top edge and 6" of a long seam open. Clip curves.

8. With right sides together, baste and sew top edge of stocking and lining together. Turn right side out.

9. Slip-stitch opening in lining closed and insert it in stocking.

10. Using overhand knot, tie a loop in the tieback unit, leaving a 3" loop and one end approximately 3" longer than the other. Sew knot to the top left corner of stocking.

Bottom and Toe

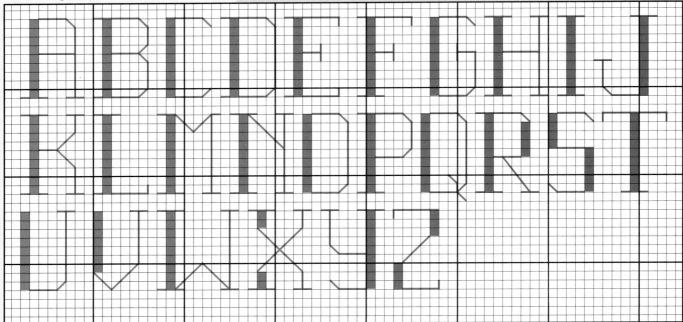

 *Making Cording*

Here's an extra idea. To customize the finishing of the piece, match the same or complementary colors, yarns, or fibers to that of your needlework.

To create a larger cord in circumference, begin with more strands than three. Try blending different yarns and fibers for a special look.

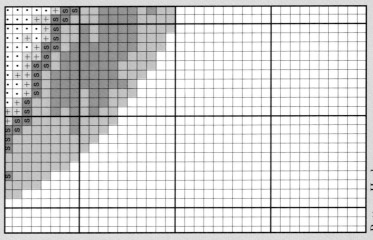

Bottom Heel

DIRECTIONS

1. Make cording using five colors of rayon metallic fiber. Use two strands of each color. If one color is desired for cording, use 10 strands of chosen color fiber.

2. For standard-size cording, calculate length of fiber needed before twisting by multiplying finished length desired by seven.

3. Fold combined fibers' entire length in thirds, and tie a knot at each end.

4. Insert a pencil in front of knots at each end. This requires two people.

5. Stand facing one another. Keep fiber taut at all times. Each person begins turning his or her pencil in a clockwise direction. Turn pencils until fiber is twisted so tightly that it begins to double back on itself just near knots. Keep taut or it will kink.

6. When twisting is complete, find approximate center of fiber.

One person holds the center, while the other person pulls the two pencils together, always keeping fiber taut.

7. After pencils are joined, the center person begins to let go, a few inches at a time. The fiber will naturally twist.

8. Upon reaching the pencils, remove pencils and tie knotted ends together.

Santa Claus

Pillow

See photo on page 85. Stitched on 10-mesh canvas, the finished design size is 7⅛" x 7⅛". The stitch count is 72 x 72. The canvas was cut 11" x 11". See graph on page 92.

OTHER CANVASES	DESIGN SIZES
12 count	6" x 6"
13 count	5½" x 5½"
18 count	4¼" x 4¼"

Cross-Stitch Picture

Pictured at right is design on page 92 converted to cross-stitch. Stitched on cream Aida 14, the finished design size is 5⅛" x 5⅛". The stitch count is 72 x 72. The fabric was cut 12" x 12".

DMC		Paternayan Persian Yarn (used for sample)	

Step 1: Continental Stitch (3 ply)

DMC		Paternayan	
White	·	260	White
746	–	715	Mustard–vy. lt.
3822		727	Autumn Yellow–ultra vy. lt.
783		724	Autumn Yellow
945		845	Salmon–vy. lt.
758	s	874	Rust–lt.
951	+	886	Ginger–ultra vy. lt.
922		884	Ginger–lt.
900		821	Tangerine–dk.
3706	□	953	Strawberry
3801		841	Salmon–dk.
498		840	Salmon–vy. dk.
3607		353	Fuchsia–lt.
718	★	352	Fuchsia
554		304	Violet–vy. lt.
208		312	Grape
327		321	Plum–vy. dk.
799		543	Cobalt Blue
798		541	Cobalt Blue–dk.
930		511	Old Blue–dk.
519		584	Sky Blue
518		583	Sky Blue–med
955		623	Shamrock–lt.
3815		662	Pine Green–med.
986		610	Hunter Green–vy. dk.
543	△	474	Toast Brown–lt.
436	○	413	Earth Brown–lt.
434		412	Earth Brown
762	H	237	Silver Gray
310	M	220	Black

Step 2: Backstitch (DMC 2 strands)

	3328	Salmon–dk. (mouth)
	3790	Beige Gray–ultra vy. dk. (mustache)
	801	Coffee Brown–dk. (nose)
	310	Black (eyes)

Pillow Finishing

MATERIALS

Completed design on 10-mesh canvas

½ yard of burgundy brocade decorator-weight fabric; matching thread

1 yard of ⅜"-wide flat multicolored decorative trim

1½ yards of 1¾"-wide multicolored fringed trim

Stuffing

DIRECTIONS
All seams are ½".

1. Block needlepoint.

2. Trim canvas ¼" from last row of stitches.

(continued on page 92)

(continued from page 91)

3. Cut two 12" square pieces of fabric for pillow front and back.

4. With design centered and facing up, baste and sew design to the front of one piece of fabric.

5. Baste and sew flat trim to

design next to stitches, covering raw canvas. Miter the trim at the corners, if needed.

6. Baste and sew fringed trim to pillow front, overlapping ends at the center bottom and rounding corners slightly.

7. With right sides together and

taking care to keep fringe out of seams, baste and sew pillow front and back together, leaving a 7" opening for turning.

8. Trim corners and turn right side out.

9. Insert stuffing into pillow. Slip-stitch opening closed.

Santa Claus

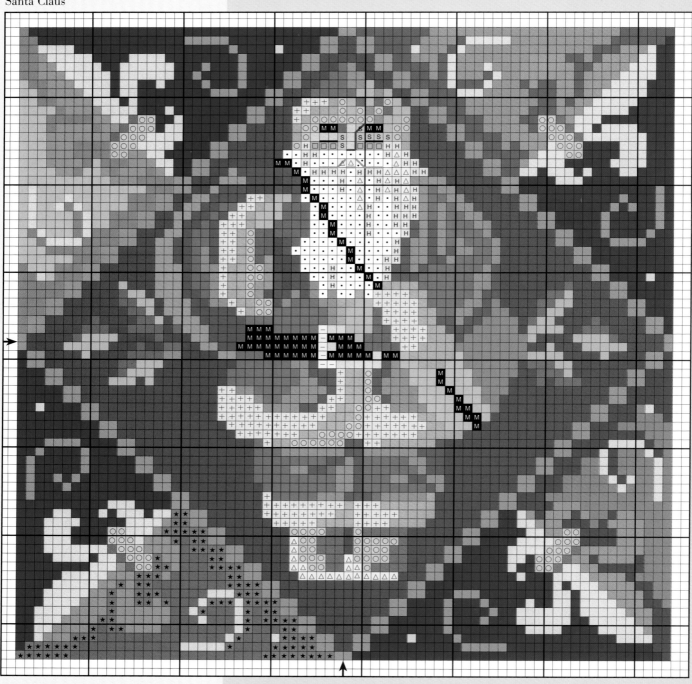

Fleur-de-lis

Stitched on 18-mesh canvas, the finished design size is 4¼" x 4¼". The stitch count is 72 x 72. The canvas was cut 10" x 10". See graph and "Coaster Finishing" instructions on page 94.

OTHER CANVASES	DESIGN SIZES
10 count	7¼" x 7¼"
12 count	6" x 6"
13 count	5½" x 5½"
14 count	5⅛" x 5⅛"

DMC		Paternayan Persian Yarn (used for sample)
		Step 1: Continental Stitch (1 ply)
3822		727 Autumn Yellow–ultra vy. lt.
783		724 Autumn Yellow
3801		841 Salmon–dk.
498		840 Salmon–vy. dk.
3607		353 Fucshia–lt.
718	★	352 Fuchsia
327		321 Plum–vy. dk.
519		584 Sky Blue

DMC		Color
518		583 Sky Blue–med.
799		543 Cobalt Blue
798		541 Cobalt Blue–dk.
986		610 Hunter Green–vy. dk.
436	▾	413 Earth Brown–lt.
434		412 Earth Brown

93

Coaster Finishing

MATERIALS—for one coaster

Completed design on 18-mesh
   canvas
4" square of medium-weight
   cardboard
4" square of tan adhesive-backed
   craft felt

DIRECTIONS

1. Block needlepoint.

2. Use binding stitch to edge
needlepoint (see "Binding Stitch"
on page 8).

3. Trim canvas 1½" from binding
stitch.

4. Center design over cardboard
and fold the raw canvas back.
Miter the corners and lace raw
edges of canvas together.

5. Peel the backing from felt and
place adhesive side down on back
of design unit, covering the raw
canvas.

Fleur-de-lis

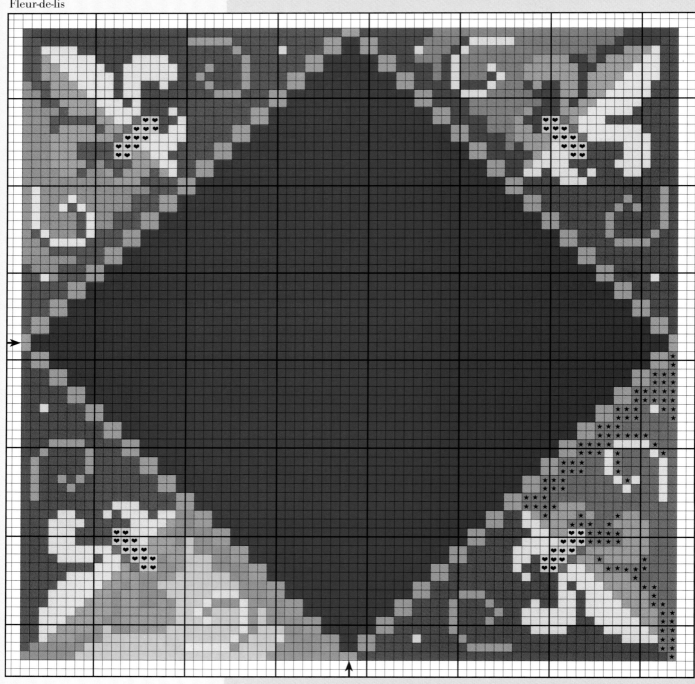

Christmas Around the World

Stitched on 18-mesh canvas, the finished design size for each ornament is 4¼" x 4¼". The stitch count for each is 72 x 72. The canvas was cut 10" x 10".

Other Canvases	Design Sizes
10 count	7¼" x 7¼"
12 count	6" x 6"
13 count	5½" x 5½"
14 count	5⅛" x 5⅛"

Ornaments Finishing

MATERIALS—for one ornament

Completed design on 18-mesh canvas
Gold 6-strand cotton floss
3"-long decorative multi-colored tassel

DIRECTIONS

1. Block needlepoint.

2. Trim canvas ½" from last row of stitches.

3. Fold raw edges of canvas under ½" and finger-press in place.

4. To form a hanger cord, cut a 30" length of gold floss. Fold in half and twist floss together. Fold in half again, letting cording twist upon itself, and knot ends together, forming a loop. Thread loop in needle, and come up through canvas at the top center point of design next to gold border.

5. Thread loop of tassel in needle, go down through canvas at center bottom point of design next to gold border, and secure it on back.

6. Fold corners of design back along the gold border, creating a diamond shape. Pin corners in place. See photo at right.

7. Use binding stitch to sew folded edges of canvas together, starting at right corner and sewing to center (see "Binding Stitch" on page 8). Repeat from the left corner to center and then from top to bottom.

Saint Nicholas Ornament

DMC		Paternayan Persian Yarn (used for sample)	
		Step 1: Continental Stitch (1 ply)	
White	·	260	White
746	–	715	Mustard–vy. lt.
3822		727	Autumn Yellow–ultra vy. lt.
783		724	Autumn Yellow
945		845	Salmon–vy. lt.
758	s	874	Rust–lt.
740	⌐	812	Sunrise–med.
900	⊞	821	Tangerine–dk.
3706	□	953	Strawberry
3801		841	Salmon–dk.
498	N	840	Salmon–vy. dk.
3607		353	Fuchsia–lt.
718	★	352	Fuchsia
3687		910	Dusty Pink–vy. dk.
799	U	543	Cobalt Blue
798	E	541	Cobalt Blue–dk.
824		550	Ice Blue–vy. dk.
930	▼	511	Old Blue–dk.
519		584	Sky Blue
518		583	Sky Blue–med
955	╱	623	Shamrock–lt.
502		663	Pine Green
3815	K	662	Pine Green–med.
986		610	Hunter Green–vy. dk.
436	○	413	Earth Brown–lt.
434	■	412	Earth Brown
422	◇	442	Golden Brown–med.
869	G	441	Golden Brown–dk.
543	△	474	Toast Brown–lt.
762	H	237	Silver Gray
310	M	220	Black

Step 2: Backstitch (DMC 2 strands)

3328	Salmon–dk. (mouth)
3790	Beige Gray–ultra vy. dk. (mustache)
801	Coffee Brown–dk. (nose)
310	Black (eyes)

Step 3: Long Loose Stitch (DMC 2 strands)

729	Old Gold–med. (drum)
3790	Beige Gray–ultra vy. dk. (drum, sailboat)
310	Black (gingerbread)

Step 4: French Knot (DMC 1 strand)

729	Old Gold–med.
3790	Beige Gray–ultra vy. dk.
310	Black

Père Noël Ornament

DMC		Paternayan Persian Yarn (used for sample)		900	+	821	Tangerine–dk.		798	E	541	Cobalt Blue–dk.
				3706	□	953	Strawberry		930	▼	511	Old Blue–dk.
		Step 1: Continental Stitch (1 ply)		3801		841	Salmon–dk.		519		584	Sky Blue
White	·	260	White	498		840	Salmon–vy. dk.		518		583	Sky Blue–med.
3822		727	Autumn Yellow–ultra vy. lt.	3607		353	Fuchsia–lt.		955	∕	623	Shamrock–lt.
783		724	Autumn Yellow	718	★	352	Fuchsia		502		663	Pine Green
945		845	Salmon–vy. lt.	3687	N	910	Dusty Pink–vy. dk.		3815	K	662	Pine Green–med.
758	S	874	Rust–lt.	327		321	Plum–vy. dk.		986		610	Hunter Green–vy. dk.
740	◪	812	Sunrise–med.	799	U	543	Cobalt Blue		436	◯	413	Earth Brown–lt.

434	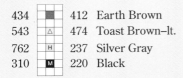	412	Earth Brown
543		474	Toast Brown–lt.
762		237	Silver Gray
310		220	Black

Step 2: Backstitch (DMC 2 strands)

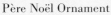 3328 Salmon–dk. (mouth)

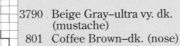 3790 Beige Gray–ultra vy. dk. (mustache)

801 Coffee Brown–dk. (nose)

310 Black (eyes, sleeves)

Step 3: Long Loose Stitch (DMC 2 strands)

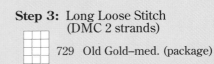 729 Old Gold–med. (package)

3328 Salmon–dk. (package)

Père Noël Ornament

98

DMC		Paternayan Persian Yarn (used for sample)								

Step 1: Continental Stitch (1 ply)

DMC		Paternayan		DMC		Paternayan		DMC		Paternayan
White	·	260 White		554		304 Violet–vy. lt.		762	H	237 Silver Gray
746	–	715 Mustard–vy. lt.		799	U	543 Cobalt Blue		310	M	220 Black
3822		727 Autumn Yellow–ultra vy. lt.		798	E	541 Cobalt Blue–dk.				
783		724 Autumn Yellow		824		550 Ice Blue–vy. dk.				
945		845 Salmon–vy. lt.		930	▼	511 Old Blue–dk.				
758	s	874 Rust–lt.		519		584 Sky Blue				
740	⌐	812 Sunrise–med.		518		583 Sky Blue–med.				
900	+	821 Tangerine–dk.		955	╱	623 Shamrock–lt.				
3706	▢	953 Strawberry		502		663 Pine Green				
3801		841 Salmon–dk.		3815	K	662 Pine Green–med.				
498		840 Salmon–vy. dk.		986		610 Hunter Green–vy. dk.				
3607		353 Fuchsia–lt.		922	×	884 Ginger–lt.				
718	★	352 Fuchsia		436	○	413 Earth Brown–lt.				
3687	N	910 Dusty Pink–vy. dk.		434		412 Earth Brown				
				422	◇	442 Golden Brown–med.				
				869	G	441 Golden Brown–dk.				
				543	△	474 Toast Brown–lt.				

Step 2: Backstitch (DMC 2 strands)

	3328	Salmon–dk. (mouth)
	3790	Beige Gray–ultra vy. dk. (mustache)
	801	Coffee Brown–dk. (nose)
	310	Black (eyes)

Step 3: Long Loose Stitch (1 ply)

922	884	Ginger–lt. (sticks)
436	413	Earth Brown–lt. (sticks)

Father Christmas Ornament

Christmas Elegance

Stocking

Stitched on 12-mesh canvas, the finished design size is 9⅝" x 15½". The stitch count is 116 x 186. The canvas was cut 12" x 18".

OTHER CANVASES	DESIGN SIZES
10 count	11⅝" x 18⅝"
13 count	8⅞" x 14¼"
14 count	8¼" x 13¼"
18 count	6½" x 10⅜"

Step 3: French Knot (1 ply)
017 HL Balger #32 Braid

Step 4: Long Stitch (1 ply)
017 HL Balger #32 Braid

DMC   Paternayan Persian Yarn (used for sample)

Step 1: Continental Stitch (2 ply)

DMC		Paternayan	
White	·	260	White
746	✳	715	Mustard–vy. lt.
677	○	754	Old Gold–lt.
744		703	Butterscotch–lt.
740		812	Sunrise–med.
947	❂	822	Tangerine–med.
351	✎	843	Salmon
3806	✕	962	Hot Pink
335	S	942	Cranberry–vy. dk.
666		970	Christmas Red–med.
326	■	940	Cranberry–deep
814		902	American Beauty–dk.
902	★	900	American Beauty–ult. vy. dk.
3727		324	Plum
552		300	Violet–dk.
3740		320	Plum–ult. vy. dk.
3761		585	Sky Blue–lt.
334		544	Cobalt Blue–lt.
3013		653	Olive Green
3012		652	Olive Green–med.
699	◢	680	Peacock Green–ult. vy. dk.
500		660	Pine Green–vy. dk.
3779		491	Flesh–med.
922		884	Ginger–lt.
920	⊻	882	Ginger–med.
839	B	461	Beige Brown–med.
762	●	237	Silver Gray
310	H	220	Black
		017	HL Balger #32 Braid

Step 2: Backstitch (2 ply)

699	╱	699	Christmas Green (DMC floss)
300	∟	300	Mahogany–vy. dk. (DMC floss)

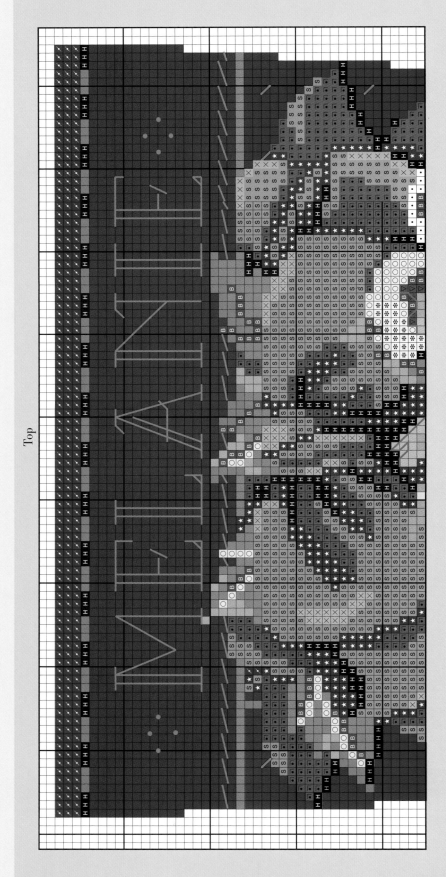

Top

MATERIALS
Completed design on 12-mesh
  canvas

½ yd. gold decorator-weight fabric;
  matching thread
42" of ¼"-wide gold metallic cord

Gold metallic cord-and-tassel
  tieback unit (28" cord with 3"-
  long tassels)

(continued on page 105)

Middle

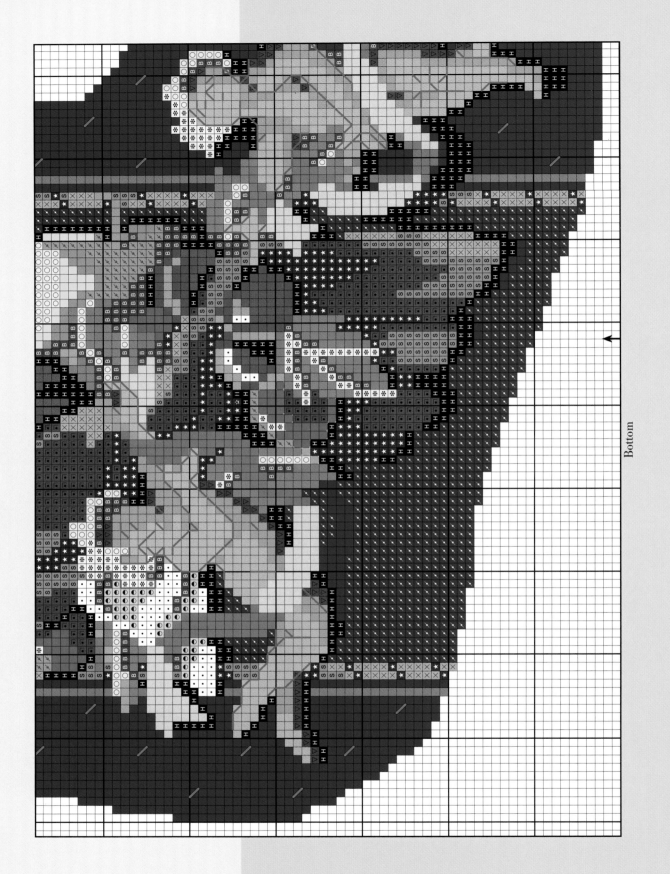

Bottom

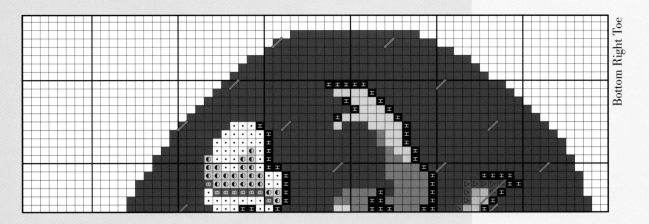

(continued from page 103)

DIRECTIONS
All seams are ½".

1. Block needlepoint.

2. Trim canvas ½" from last row of stitches around stocking.

3. Using design as pattern, cut three pieces of decorator fabric for stocking lining and back.

4. With right sides together, baste and sew one decorator fabric piece to the stocking, leaving the top edge open. Clip curves and turn right side out.

5. Slip-stitch 42" length of gold cord in seam, hiding ends inside stocking.

6. With right sides together, baste and sew remaining fabric pieces together to make a lining, leaving the top edge and 6" of a long seam open. Clip curves.

7. With right sides together, baste and sew top edge of stocking and lining together. Turn right side out.

8. Slip-stitch opening in lining closed and insert it in stocking.

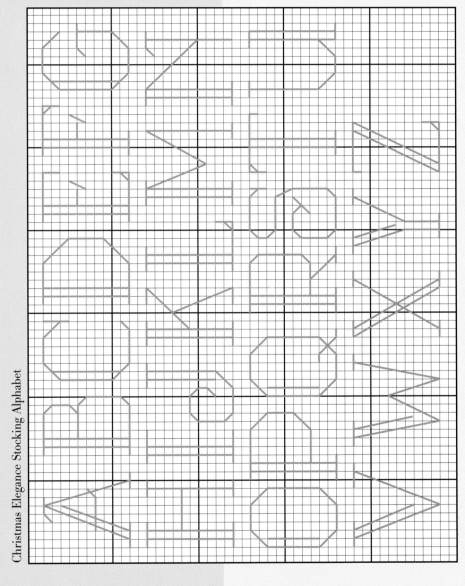

9. Using overhand knot, tie a loop in the tieback unit, leaving a 3" loop and one end about 3" longer than the other. Sew knot to the top left corner of stocking.

Picture

Stitched on 12-mesh canvas, the finished design size is 12" x 12". The stitch count is 144 x 144. The canvas was cut 18" x 18". See photo on page 102.

OTHER CANVASES	DESIGN SIZES
10 count	14⅜" x 14⅜"
13 count	11⅛" x 11⅛"
14 count	10¼" x 10¼"
18 count	8" x 8"

DMC		Paternayan Persian Yarn (used for sample)	

Step 1: Continental Stitch (2 ply)

White	·	260	White
746	*	715	Mustard–vy. lt.
677	○	754	Old Gold–lt.
744		703	Butterscotch–lt.
740		812	Sunrise–med.
947		822	Tangerine–med.
351	✗	843	Salmon
3806	✕	962	Hot Pink
335	s	942	Cranberry–vy.dk.
666		970	Christmas Red–med.
326		940	Cranberry–deep
902	★	900	American Beauty–ultra vy. dk.
3727		324	Plum
552		300	Violet–dk.
3740		320	Plum–ultra vy. dk.
3761		585	Sky Blue–lt.
334		544	Cobalt Blue–lt.
3013		653	Olive Green
3012		652	Olive Green–med.
699		680	Peacock Green–ultra vy. lt.
500		660	Pine Green–vy. dk.
3779		491	Flesh–med.
922		884	Ginger–lt.
920		882	Ginger–med.
839	B	461	Beige Brown–med.
762	●	237	Silver Gray
310	H	220	Black
		017	HL Balger #32 Braid

Step 2: Backstitch (2 strands)

699		699	Christmas Green (DMC floss)
300		300	Mahogany–vy. dk.

Step 3: Long Stitch (1 ply)

		017	HL Balger #32 Braid
922		884	Ginger–lt.

Top Left

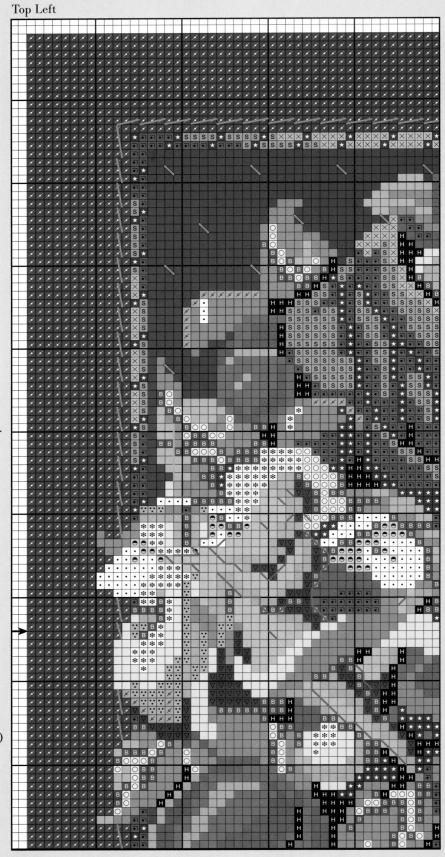

Top Center

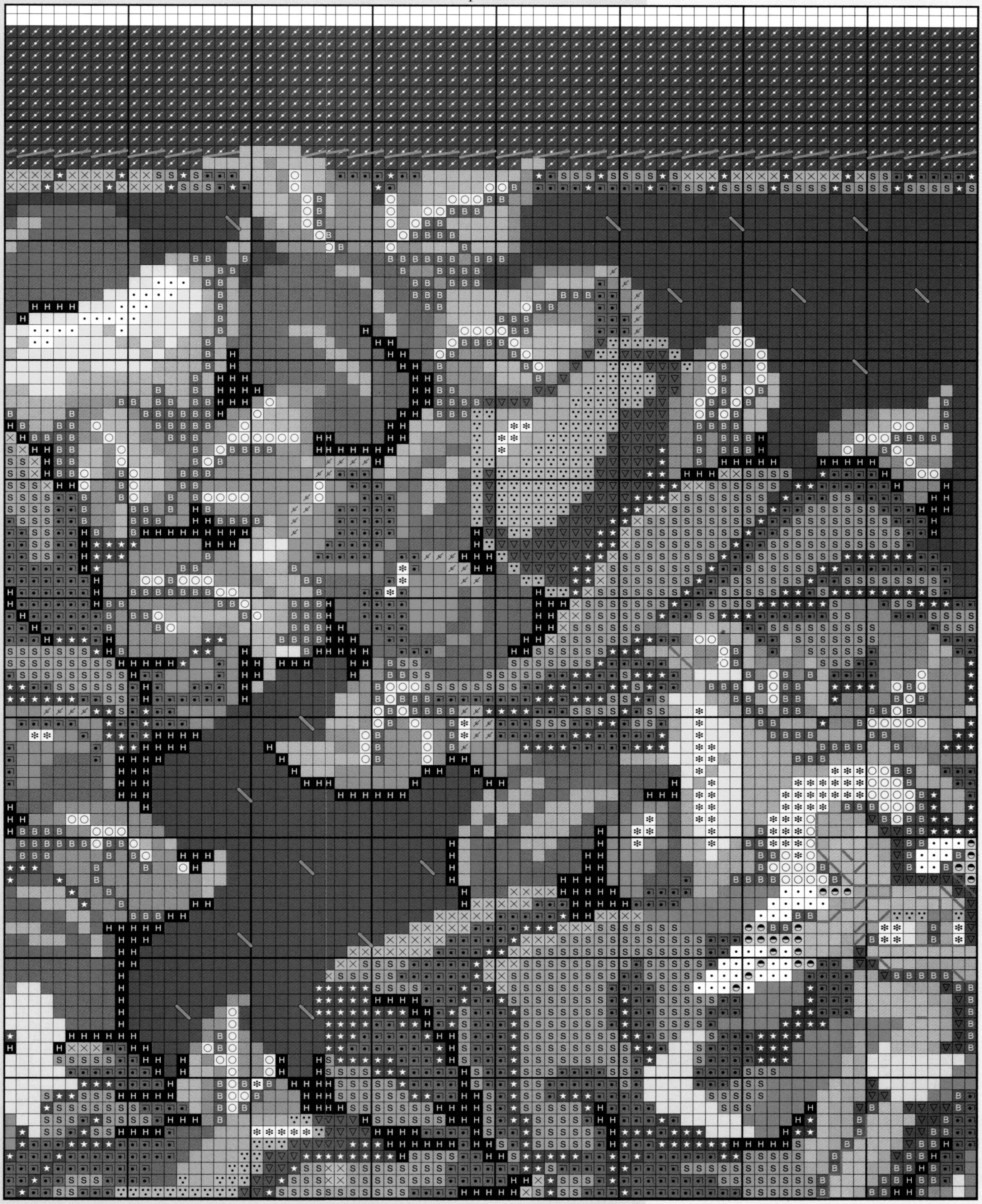

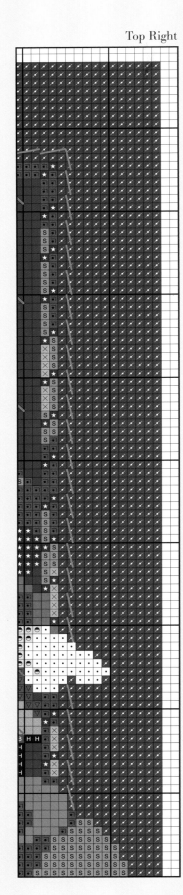

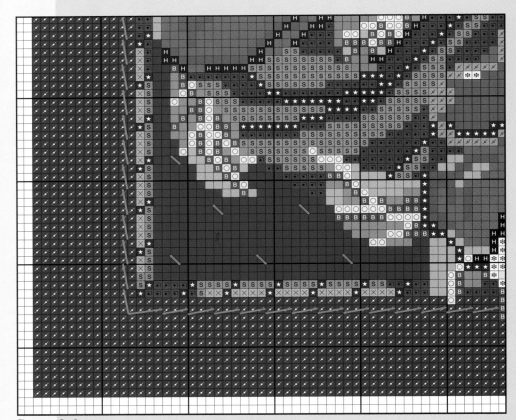

Bottom Left

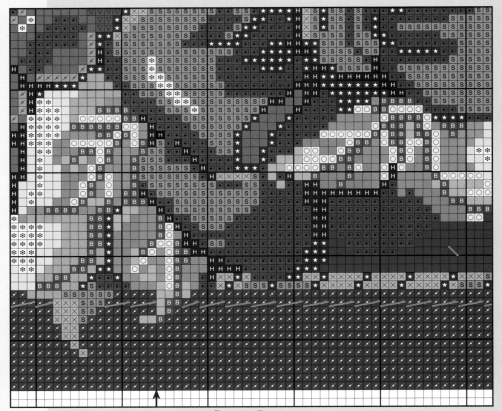

Bottom Center

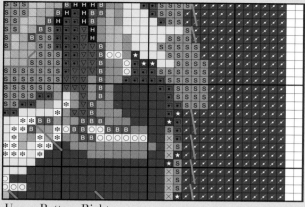

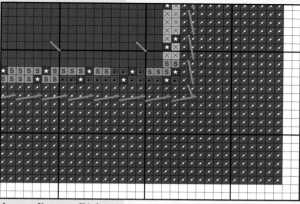

Upper Bottom Right

Lower Bottom Right

Coasters

Stitched on 12-mesh canvas, the finished design size for each coaster is 4¼" x 4¼". The stitch count for each is 47 x 47. The canvas for each was cut 8" x 8".

OTHER CANVASES	DESIGN SIZES
10 count	4¾" x 4¾"
13 count	3⅝" x 3⅝"
14 count	3⅜" x 3⅜"
18 count	2⅝" x 2⅝"

Bow-tied Berries

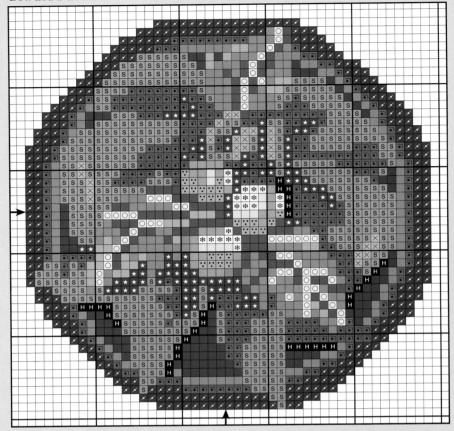

DMC	Paternayan Persian Yarn (used for sample)	

Step 1: Continental Stitch (2 ply)

		DMC		
White	·	260	White
746	✳	715	Mustard–vy. lt.
677	○	754	Old Gold–lt.
744		703	Butterscotch–lt.
740		812	Sunrise–med.
947	⠇	822	Tangerine–med.
351	✗	843	Salmon
3806	✕	962	Hot Pink
335	s	942	Cranberry–vy. dk.
666		970	Christmas Red–med.
326	⊡	940	Cranberry–deep
902	★	900	American Beauty–ult.vy. dk.
3727		324	Plum
552		300	Violet–dk.
3740		320	Plum–ultra vy. dk.
3761		585	Sky Blue–lt.
3013		653	Olive Green
3012		652	Olive Green–med.
699	✺	680	Peacock Green–ult. vy. dk.
500		660	Pine Green–vy. dk.
922		884	Ginger–lt.
920	▽	882	Ginger–med.
839		461	Beige Brown–med.
310	H	220	Black
		017	HL Balger #32 Braid

Step 2: Long Loose Stitch (1 ply)

839	╱	461	Beige Brown–med.

Pears & Cherries

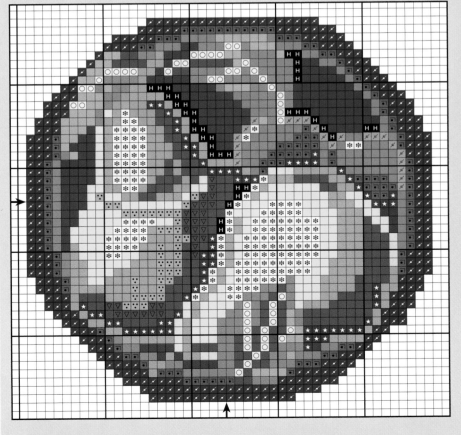

Peach, Plum & Cherries

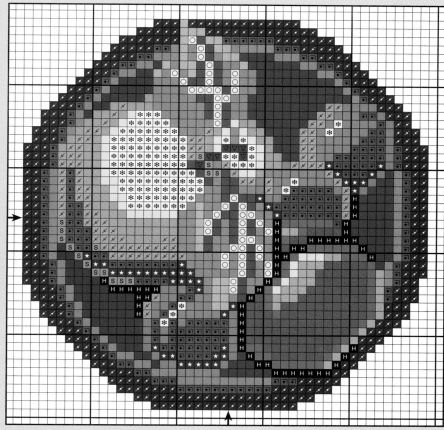

Plums & Cherries

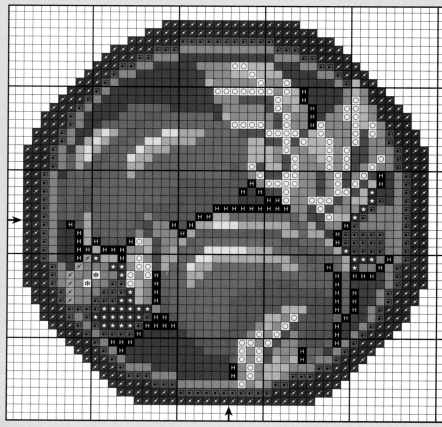

MATERIALS—for one coaster

Completed design on 12-mesh
   canvas
4" square of medium-weight
   cardboard
4" square of tan adhesive-backed
   craft felt
12" of ⅛"-wide burgundy cord

DIRECTIONS
All seams are ½".

1. Block needlepoint.

2. Using enlarged Elegance
Coaster Pattern on page 112, trim
canvas to Canvas Cut Line.

3. Using pattern, cut Cardboard
Form from cardboard.

4. Center design over cardboard,
and fold the raw canvas back.
Miter the corners, and lace raw
edges of canvas together.

5. Peel the backing from felt, and
place adhesive side down on back
of design unit, covering the raw
canvas.

6. Slip-stitch burgundy cord in
seam, overlapping ends.

Elegance Coaster Pattern

From page 111. Enlarge 145%.

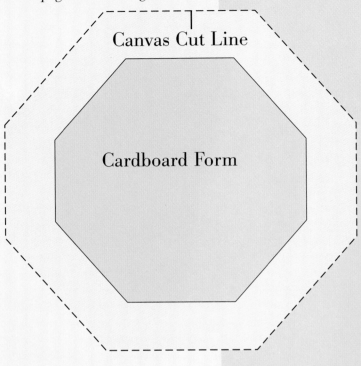

Canvas Cut Line

Cardboard Form

Metric Equivalency Chart

MM-Millimetres   CM-Centimetres

INCHES TO MILLIMETRES AND CENTIMETRES

INCHES	MM	CM	INCHES	CM
⅛	3	0.3	9	22.9
¼	6	0.6	10	25.4
½	13	1.3	12	30.5
⅝	16	1.6	13	33.0
¾	19	1.9	14	35.6
⅞	22	2.2	15	38.1
1	25	2.5	16	40.6
1¼	32	3.2	17	43.2
1½	38	3.8	18	45.7
1¾	44	4.4	19	48.3
2	51	5.1	20	50.8
2½	64	6.4	21	53.3
3	76	7.6	22	55.9
3½	89	8.9	23	58.4
4	102	10.2	24	61.0
4½	114	11.4	25	63.5
5	127	12.7	26	66.0
6	152	15.2	27	68.6
7	178	17.8	28	71.1
8	203	20.3	29	73.7

YARDS	METRES	YARDS	METRES
⅛	0.11	⅞	0.80
¼	0.23	1	0.91
⅜	0.34	2	1.83
½	0.46	3	2.74
⅝	0.57	4	3.66
¾	0.69	5	4.57

Index